Twitter Top Success Secrets and Best practices: Twitter Experts Share The World's Greatest Tips

Twitter Success Secrets

Twitter Success Secrets

There has never been a Twitter Guide like this.

Success Secrets is *not* about the ins and outs of Twitter. Instead, it answers the top questions that we are asked and those we come across in forums, our consultancy and education programs.

It tells you exactly how to deal with those questions, with tips that have never before been offered in print.

This book is also *not* about Twitter's best practice and standards details. Instead, it introduces everything you want to know to be successful with Twitter.

Table of Contents

Tweet yourself to Twitter

By Steve Nichols

Have you heard of Twitter? Don't worry, if you haven't you soon will. The endless search for new social networking tools has seen the rise of MySpace, Facebook and LinkedIn among others. Twitter is just one of these new tools, but has been predicted by TIME Magazine to become the next killer application on the net.

So what is all the fuss about?

Twitter is a micro-blogging tool; a little like the status updates on Facebook where you can add a short two-line piece about what you are up too. These are surprisingly useful as you can see at a glance what your friends and colleagues are doing. For example, as I sit here writing this one friend's car has just been rear-ended, another has driven across country for an "adventure", a friend has just got back in the country after being away for four weeks and fellow hack Geoff is just coming back from Sri Lanka.

Now, whether you find this information useful or just a load of old twaddle will probably give you a clue as to whether you will find Twitter interesting.

In its own words, "Twitter allows you to share bite-sized updates (or 'tweets') about your life."

The first step is to go to www.twitter.com and sign up for a free account. Then you need to find out which of your friends are actually on Twitter. Once you have found some you can "follow" them, getting a web-page of their updates as they happen.

These updates are 140 characters or less and are short and succinct, just like the Facebook status updates.

So why, I hear you say, should I be interested in Twitter, if it only offers a small portion of what Facebook does?

Well, Twitter goes a little bit further than Facebook in that you can follow these updates via the Twitter website, via a browser plug-in, your mobile phone or instant messaging.

This is where Twitter scores - but only if you have contacts who actually use Twitter in the first place. Once you sign up and if you have an account with a major e-mail provider like Google mail, Hotmail or Yahoo you can let Twitter search your contacts to see if any of them use the system. This didn't seem to work too well for me, on any of the e-mail accounts that I tried.

You can also search by location and/or invite or colleagues friends via e-mail.

If this is still leaving you cold, let me show you how people are using it. Barack Obama is a Twitter fan. His site at http://twitter.com/BarackObama lets people keep up to date with where he is and what he is up to. In fact, he has more than 84,000 followers.

The Los Angeles Fire Department put the technology to use during the October 2007 California wildfires and Twitter was used by NASA to keep people up to date with news of the discovery of what appeared to be water ice on Mars by the Phoenix Mars Lander.

When an American student was arrested in Egypt, he managed to send a brief text with a single word - "ARRESTED" - which was picked up around the world via Twitter and led quickly to his release, helped by a lawyer hired by his university back in the US.

So how could you use Twitter? Perhaps you could use it to link your communications professionals around the globe. Or perhaps put a human face on your CEO.

As always, the tool is there. You just need to work out if and how it could help you.

ENDS

About the Author

Steve Nichols' TechNotes blog is at http://infotechcomms.blogspot.com/ and is described as a regular ramble that tries to demystify technology and help people get to grips with new-fangled gizmos, such as the internet, streaming audio/video, DTP and digital imaging. You can get it via RSS at http://infotechcomms.blogspot.com/atom.xml

Getting Started With Twitter

By Wesley Craig Green

There's a new web application on the block that has everyone talking and it goes by the name of Twitter. Twitter is fast becoming one of the more popular methods for communicating online and has a large number of loyal followers who stick with it despite the growing pains and competitors. While this article won't cover everything possible with Twitter, it will give you a good starting point on how to start using it and how you can use it for your business.

What Is This Twitter You Speak Of?

So what is Twitter and how can it be of benefit to you or your business? Twitter is a free online micro-blogging application which gives you the ability to send out short messages (up to 140 characters) called "tweets" to people who are following you on Twitter.

You can send tweets either through your computer or by using your cell phone via a text message. These tweets/messages can be about anything you want and they can include links, as well.

Making Twitter even more useful is the ability to send a direct message to someone you are following (this is done by entering @username at the beginning of your message) or replying to someone's tweet with your own. You would be surprised how common it is to reply to someone's message then to have someone who is either following you or the person you sent the reply to reply to your initial message and so on.

People can follow you and your tweets by first signing-up for their own free Twitter account at the Twitter site then adding you to their list of people they are following. Once you have created your account, you can either check your Twitter page (your own personal page which appears after you sign-in at the Twitter home page) for any of your friend's new messages or you can send out your own. But it is much easier, in my opinion, to use one of the many online or desktop applications which give you the ability to do all of this and more.

Twitter As A Communication Tool

Twitter is a quick and easy way to communicate with family, friends, business associates, and also within a company setting. Being an online service, Twitter is available to anyone with online access. All you have to do is login to your account through any number of third-party applications developed for Twitter or through the Twitter site and you are ready to go.

Within a company setting, employees could have a Twitter account created for them with the option to have their messages protected. This means only people they (or you or the person in charge of creating the Twitter accounts) approve will be able to send and receive messages from them. The same thing could be done using an instant message program but with Twitter, there would be no software to install and it would be accessible from anywhere with an online connection. Additionally, the person who is in charge of the Twitter accounts will have the power to control who is and who isn't part of this private Twitter network.

Even though there are tons of online communication applications available, Twitter can also be used as a way for people who are collaborating on a project to stay in touch with one another regardless of where they are. And depending on which third-party application they are using to Twitter with, these conversations can be saved for future reference. There are even some third-party apps which you can use to send files up to 10MB to anyone you are following as long as they are using the same application, that is. Still, a handy feature to have and one which may become a feature of Twitter if there's a big enough demand for it.

Marketing With Twitter

Here in lies the great thing about Twitter from a business perspective: the marketing potential it offers users. Sure, it is great to send messages and chat using Twitter, but it can also be a great marketing tool if used correctly. Have some breaking news you want to get out quickly? Send it out as a Tweet. Made an important update to your blog or web site? Let people know about it instantly with a Tweet.

Want to promote your project, book, movie, whatever by giving away a free download or preview? Send out a Tweet with a URL to the free download. Only want to market something to certain individuals you are following? Simply enter their username preceded by the "@" and you are set.

Another simple marketing tool available with Twitter is the ability to befriend people who are following someone you already follow. While this practice could backfire on you if you begin to add everyone you find following someone you are following, be picky and just befriend those who either share similar tastes that you do or work in the same field as you or already follow many of the same people you do. Otherwise, you could come off as a spammer which will be a hard image to shake.

Twitter Now And Beyond

Twitter represents a fundamental change in the way people communicate online. There have always been instant messengers and they have their place and purpose but they don't offer the one thing which sets Twitter apart and that is the ability to instantly communicate with either a couple of people or potentially thousands without the need for proprietary software. No need to download this piece of software in order to communicate with this person or that organization.

Much like how blogging has become a staple of today's society, Twitter and "twittering" is on the same path to becoming ingrained in today's culture despite only being around for less than two years. So simple in its execution, powerful in the marketing opportunities it offers, and ease of use, Twitter will be one of the top web technologies to gain worldwide prominence in 2008.

If you like, you can follow me on Twitter by going to http://twitter.com/GeekEntrepreneu and click on the Follow button.

About the Author

Wesley Craig Green is The Geek Entrepreneur, an entrepreneur who is a publisher, owner of an online classified ads network of sites, two web sites focusing on independent and digital comics and graphic novels. You can check out my personal blog, Geek Entrepreneur which is dedicated to entrepreneurship, blogging, inspiration, technology, and small business.

5 Reasons Why Twitter Social Networking Is The Next Big Thing

By Quang Van

If you haven't heard of Twitter you should. I know Twitter is popular on the west coast, but haven't reach mainstream yet.

But the reasons why Twitter will be the next big thing is the same reasons why anything becomes popular.

Here's the top 5 reasons.

1) It is easy to use. Nothing complicated ever became popular. At least not until it became easy to use.

Twitter is very easy to use. All you basically have to do is, tell it "What You Are Doing?"

2) Texting is very popular. Are you around young people? Young people barely use the phone anymore.

Cell phones are so, 2000....

These days the mobile communication of choice is texting.

The same reasons why texting is popular so will twitter. Twitter is basically the online version of texting.

3) Highly adaptable. Why is RSS so popular? Because of its simple context and it's adaptability.

These days RSS is used for everything. From Podcasts, to newsfeeds... to video feeds, to friend feeds.

To stream flickr pictures, web blogs and everything in between. It is very adaptable.

This is the same reason Twitter will be popular. It could be used for anything. It is very simple, therefore it could be used for multiple purposes.

4) People are nosy... Yes, people always what to know what other people are doing.

There are people who go on AIM (aol instant messenger) just to read people's "Away Messages".

That's right, they go onto a communication platform, not to communicate, but to just read what other people are doing.

Twitter is basically AIM away messages... it's what people want, stripped of the non-essential stuff.

5) Twitter will connect people. A weird phenomenon on Twitter is, special groups dedicated to a particular purpose forming on Twitter.

People join the group, and follow one another.

These days when one works in lonely cubicles or home offices, it's nice to connect to other people.

About the Author

To learn more about twitter, upcoming social networks and get your free report, click here.

Make Money Business Opportunity Online

3-Ways To Twitter Traffic-Generate Twitter Traffic Fast

By Skeeter Hansen, Al Ferretti, Jim Grygar

Only recently Internet marketers all over started realizing the traffic generation explosion power of this social networking/micro-blogging tool we know as Twitter. Twitter is a great tool to get tons of traffic, but there are specific rules to follow to get success in it, as with other social networking sites:

1. Don't Sell or Spam! Don't pitch anything heavily or try to over sell on Twitter. Sure, maybe you can do it once in a while with a little link to your sales page, but do it like only 1 out of every 20 posts. You do not want to heavily pitch products here to your friends, because it's rude and considered spam.

2. Shoot For Syndication One of the big pluses is that you can easily ask people to syndicate your content for you or vote for your content. You can ask people to check out your blog posts, and some people might link back to it if your content is good, so that drives traffic for you. If you use social media sites like Digg and Stumble Upon, you can ask your friends to vote your content, and that will again give you more exposure online.

3. Build Relationships Build business relationships using Twitter by posting comments on other people's blog and articles. This is a great tool to use for generating traffic to your web sites. You can also easily post a 2 or 3 line note a few seconds after logging into Twitter. Many people have formed powerful joint venture relationships just by using Twitter alone.

These are 3 ways that http://www.traffic-generation-explosion.com makes the most of Twitter to reel in traffic. Author: Al Ferretti, Jim Grygar, Skeeter Hansen

About the Author

The days of building a website and just waiting for people to come are over. Would you agree an online business lives or dies based on how much traffic it gets? I've sold countless products online and want to show you through my successes and failures what works.

How to Use Twitter as a Marketing Tool

By Joan Yankowitz

Are you using Twitter yet? More and more Internet market-ers are using Twitter as a marketing/public relations tool, and I don't think we've even tapped the surface. Here are some ways to use Twitter to help grow your business. Build Your Network

- Decide whether you want to market yourself or your com-pany. - Personalize your account by setting up your profile - Find friends to follow through your email contacts - Find other top Twitter users to follow in your niche - Follow thought-leaders and the people thought-leaders follow (you can always un-follow them) - Get involved in networks where very thoughtful conversations are happening - Get involved in conversations already happening

Engage With Your Community

- Jump into the conversation - remember that it's a discus-sion, not a broadcast tool - Follow people who follow you - Publish helpful content - give people a reason to follow you - Use Twitter for events - Take online relationships to an offline "Tweet up" - Don't "tweet" your intimate personal information. Be discreet Track and Analyze

- Measure your Twitter account's influence - Measure your ongoing sales activity

Use Tools

- Set up your blog feed to automatically send posts to Twit-ter

Don't Spam or Abuse

- Be respectful and don't "over-tweet" - Don't use links that point to phishing sites, malware, or other harmful material - "Tweet" about other things than your business - Don't follow a large number of people in a short amount of time - the number of followers is small compared to number of people following - Don't "re-tweet" (poach other users' updates)

It's easy and free to set up your Twitter account. Use the tips above and you will get a lot out of Twitter and grow your business social network. Happy tweeting!

About the Author

Joan Yankowitz is the Internet Marketing Maven. Get her straight talk on Internet Marketing and Blogging free tools, best resources, product reviews, and important trends at The Internet Marketing Maven right now!

Is Twitter Useful for Business?

By Richard Allen

One of the newest social networking sites is Twitter. It sounds like a movement birds make. In fact it is a quick way to send messages to your favorite people via the Internet. Due to its popularity with people all over the world, many entrepreneurs wonder if Twitter can actually help them grow their business. But is it twitter useful.

In order to answer that question we first need to find out what exactly Twitter is? It is a social networking site which allows people to keep in touch with friends, family, and others. Through a series of short posts, important information is sent to a person's followers. Those short posts are called "tweets."

Twitter has been used by people to send messages to their friends. The posts can be 140 characters long at most, which allows for quick, precise exchanges of information. If you wanted to let your family know that the reunion this year is in Baton Rouge, Louisiana, and they needed to volunteer to do something, it would be easy to send them all a tweet at one time. When someone logs into their Twitter account or views your Twitter profile page, they would then see the message. They can then respond to you by posting a tweet of their own.

Twitter is real time communication for people who need to contact others right away. Some wondered if Twitter was just a fancy way of texting someone on the computer. Send a tweet to your husband to say dinner is moved to 7:30. Tell a girlfriend you've just bought that blouse you saw last week. If you only want to allow certain people to see the messages you are sending, you can easily mark your profile and updates as private.

Although many use Twitter as a more personal way to communicate, even more treat it as a virtual water cooler to connect with all types of people the world over. It seems as if tweeting would get boring after a while. Not so. It is very popular with talkative friends you could be tweeted to death in a matter of days. Many actually find themselves losing precious time in their day chit-chatting with those with similar interests.

For the skeptical folks who want to know if tweeting will eventually tank, businesses have found a use for the social network that can increase their utilization and visibility on the Internet. First, let's say that you have an office of fifty employees. Sending a memo every time there is a big announcement creates a lot of paper to file or leave for the trash man.

Businesses can now use protected Twitter messages to keep employees updated on departmental changes as well as company-wide agendas. Employees can subscribe to the company feed set up on Twitter. Whenever there is something important posted, they will be notified.

The same goes for small one-owner and Internet businesses and their customers. Customers can subscribe to the company feed to learn about new products and other useful information. New businesses can create interesting tweets that produce interest and can be re-posted by others to help get the business or owner noticed.

Twitter fills a niche in the social networking sector and is here to stay. Businesses have found a way to make Twitter work to their advantage, whether they are work at home mom's longing for adult interaction or reaching out to a broader audience to increase profit.

This answers our question 'Is Twitter useful ' Yes it is.

Thanks For Reading

Richard

About the Author

No Cost Two Hour Traffic Seminar From A Five Figure A Day Marketer Without traffic you won't make any cash. With the right knowledge you can generate literally as many visitors as you want. Five figure daily returns are within reach if you watch this two hour online seminar. And it won't cost you a penny to view it, or to put the traffic strategies into action http://tinyurl.com/6bxpav

Twitter Tweets Value For Online Marketers

By David Schaefer

What is Twitter? Well, on the Twitter login page it is introduced as: a service for friends, family, and co-workers to communicate and stay connected through the exchange of quick, frequent answers to one simple question: What are you doing?

The concept of Twitter at first glance appears to offer a very unique method of communicating with people for casual banter. However, if you are marketing in any way on the Internet, this can be a powerful platform for providing information and for generating traffic.

When entering a message (known as a Tweet), the user is forced to communicate effectively, because the content is limited to 140 characters. It does not take long to figure out how to concisely get your Tweet across.

If Twitter is new to you, perhaps you have not yet grasped its true potential. It definitely has to be one of the best free traffic generators on the Internet. Its simplicity and accessibility has made this tool extremely attractive to over two million users, and that figure seems to be growing exponentially.

Once you register to participate on Twitter (http://twitter.com), you will begin to follow other Twitterers. But, the real key for you as a marketer is to generate your own followers. Thus, giving you the opportunity to get your message out quickly and easily.

As with any marketing headline, the goal of the Tweet is to capture the reader's attention and lead them to where your moneymaker content is located (sales page, opt-in, article, etc). Within your 140 characters you hopefully entice the reader and provide a short hyperlink.

Beyond the linked message area, the perks of this site are multifaceted. The page begins with an automatic welcome that introduces you to the reader and invites them to become a follower. Next, in a personal information area in the upper right corner of the page you can embed a link to a web page and provide a brief bio.

Of course, if you are going to encourage folks to follow you (or to retain followers), your Tweets need to offer value. For the Internet marketer there can sometimes be a fine line between responsibly leading someone to more information or using a platform to blatantly spam an unwanted message.

Take the opportunity to promote your Twitter page whenever possible. Place your Twitter link on your website, blog, ezine, article signature box, and so on. For example, this is my link: http://twitter.com/davidschaefer, and I encourage you to become a follower.

Twitter.com includes a few more features not mentioned here - just visit the help section. And, everyday creative entrepreneurs are offering new products and services to independently support and expand the use of Twitter. The most important point is to take advantage of Twitters simplicity, effectiveness, and potential marketing reach.

About the Author

David Schaefer is a success coach and writes on the topics of personal development and Internet marketing. He offers a FREE Report on how to profit from a Ready-Made Internet Marketing Plan at http://InfiniteIncomePlanRevealed.com.

For more articles by Dr. Schaefer visit http://DiscoverMillionDollarDesire.com/blog and follow him at http://twitter.com/davidschaefer.

How to Use Twitter to Explode Your Network Marketing Business

By Hiro Kaneko

I recently received an email from Mike Dillard giving me his Twitter URL. In fact, he sent the email and invited all the people on his Magnetic Sponsoring email list.

Why would he do that?

More importantly, why should YOU also be using Twitter for your Network Marketing business?

Twitter, as many of you may already know, is basically a free social networking and micro-blogging service that can be used to stay in touch and keeping up with friends no matter where you are or what you're doing.

Twitter allows its users (a.k.a. twits) to send updates (otherwise known as tweets) which are text based posts of up to 140 characters in length. You can get instant updates over your mobile phone, or can just check on the web. You get to choose how connected you want to be.

Now, what's this got to do with your Network Marketing business?

Good question.

Well, it's all about staying connected to your audience, building and maintaining relationship by continued communication. This is one of the key elements in the new 'attraction marketing' model where you attract people to you by providing value and sharing your expertise to people.

Twitter makes this continued connection very easy to do.

Another good thing about using Twitter is, and one of the reasons why Mike Dillard decided to invite everyone on his Magnetic Sponsoring email list, is that he'll be able to send people links to every new issue of his Magnetic Sponsoring Newsletter without having to worry about getting through the spam filters.

Here's is how it works.

You give people your Twitter URL, just like Mike Dillard did.

You can send yours out to your email list, give it out via blogs, MySpace, Facebook, etc. For example, mine is http://twitter.com/hirokaneko.

When someone clicks on the link and goes to the page, he or she can choose to either follow you or leave the site without choosing to follow you.

If someone chooses to follow you, he or she will be seeing your updates... about anything. It's kind of similar to those updates you see on Facebook.

In essence, you can keep in touch with more people about anything. And the more people see you and hear from you, the more likely the audience will buy from you or want to know more about what you offer.

If you don't have a Twitter account yet, you can get one there as well. Don't miss the trend!

And now I would like to invite you to sign up for your free "7-Day Internet Network Marketing e-course" when you go to www.HiroKaneko.com

31

From Hiro Kaneko - the Internet Network Marketing Guy and the owner of www.MLMOnlineLeadSystem.com

About the Author

Hiro is an Online Marketing & Business Coach. He works with networkers, from beginners and leaders, who seek a crash course in the new attraction-based marketing model. He shares the tools and knowledge to help entrepreneurs get positioned as experts and true solutions providers.

Visit his blog for tons of helpful Internet Network Marketing tips, best practices, and business-building strategies: http://HiroKaneko.com.

Maximizing Your 140 Characters on Twitter

By Matthew Bredel

Are you Twittering yet? Those new to Twitter might not really 'get' what it this social marketing tool is at first but as soon as you find some people to follow and get people following you, you're going to see the potential. Micro blogging is mini blogging and it can pack a wallop of a punch in terms of social networking and marketing because of the potential for followers who could pay attention to everything you have to say! Woo people with credit cards in their hand and you are golden!

What's interesting is how many people on the micro blogging platform are being sold something constantly and don't even realize it because they're just participating in an online discussion. Those discussions lead to links being clicked on and buzz being spread and ultimately, to people making money!

If you want to make money online and think you don't have time for a tool with 140 characters and a lot of idle chit chat, you're leaving money on the table! Look at Twitter and see all the potential.

Follow and Be Followed

Twitter only works if you're following people and they're following you. If you've joined and done nothing with your profile, it's not going to do anything for you. Follow and be followed. One doesn't work well without the other. Unless you're super famous, people won't stay on your follower list unless they feel like you're listening to them. If you're an online guru with a lot of clout people might not really care if you're on their list because they still want to know what you're saying but if you're going to use the tool, you need to be prepared to converse with the little people and avoid elitism. That's not to say you have to follow every single person that clicks on your name, though. There's a fair bit of Twitter spam going on so you'll want to be a little bit choosy about whether you follow someone or not. And, that tells you right there what you shouldn't use Twitter for. Spammers quickly get ignored with this tool.

Twitter Tools

Because Twitter is a pretty basic tool, there are a lot of advantages to using some of the free tools that exist to enhance the Twitter experience. There are dozens of tools that help you get Twitter doing what you want or help you mine the user base for information. Tools like Tweetdeck, Twhirl, TwitterFox, Tweet-Beep, Hashtags, Twittermail, Twitterly and more all have varying features and benefits that can help you maximize the earning potential.

Success from Reciprocity

Reciprocity is key to success on this social marketing tool. Because it's a virtual water cooler environment, you need to be a positive contributor in order to gain benefits from it. After you find a group to follow and get some people to follow you, you need to converse, you need to provide value and you should establish yourself as a valuable person to follow. Then, people will do things like: click your URL, re-tweet your interesting tweets, tell others to follow you, write @before your username so their followers can see you might be worth following, social bookmarking your interesting tweets, digging your URLs and more. See how this tool can help you?

About the Author

Are you interested in making http://www.thewebreviewer.com/articles/article/113/make-money-with-social-marketing.htm money with Twitter? Learn more social marketing potential and about making money with Twitter at Tru-Social-Guru and TheWebReviewer.

10 Secrets to Using Twitter to Attract More Followers and Get More Clients

By Donna Gunter

Copyright (c) 2008 OnlineBizU.com

I do wonder at times if some Twitter users have any time to get any work done. Several of the more prolific ones that I follow swear they spend no more than 30 minutes a day on Twitter, but I really find that hard to believe. Many times it seems they are twittering just to say something, like "Good morning Twitterverse" when they begin their day, give more details than I want to know about what they had for lunch, what their children said to them, or when they take a nap.

I realize that this is part of the "like, know, and trust" process that enables people to get to know each other, but sometimes it's simply too much information..LOL. I'm Twittering primarily to market my business. Consequently, I try and limit my personal twitters to no more than 2 per day. My clients, who create Twitter accounts for marketing, as well, tell me, "I'm signed up. Now what in the world do I Twitter about? How do I market my business with this tool?"

Here are 10 strategies that I use regularly to marketing my business and my expertise via Twitter. Remember, you have only 140 characters for your tweet (Twitter post).

1. How you're helping clients. Talk about specific ways that your business helps clients and use their Twitter ID if you have their permission, i.e. "Just finished @clientname brainstorm great Internet marketing plan for 2009" or "Finally finished setting up

QuickBooks for local hardware store -- now they can invoice their clients"

2. What you're doing in your own business. This is a perfect time to tell others when you're blogging, writing an article, creating your weekly ezine, recording your podcast, i.e. "Had great interview with Jane Smith today on speaking to grow your biz. Great ideas! Subscribe to podcast & listen here <URL here>"

3. Useful tool or resource you've found. I run across these all the time in my daily activities, and Twitter is a perfect place to share,. i.e. "Found great new Firefox plug-in to monitor & check multiple Gmail accounts at same time at <URL here>" or "Read great blog post on working at home with kids under 5 at (URL here)"

4. Ask a question. Need some ideas or some quick brainstorming? Twitter is an ideal place to gather opinions, i.e. "Help! Desperately seeking new laser printer. Recommendations?" or "How do I find training organizations online?"

5. Conduct a survey. What do your Tweeps think about a particular issue? Ask them via Twitter, i.e. "Quick poll: Do you get more clients from Facebook or Twitter? Respond at (URL here)"

6. Report on live events. The latest Twitter trend seems to be tweeting what's happening at conferences or workshops. In order for Twitter users to follow a particular event, it's usually referred to by a name preceded by a # sign, as in #JVAlert, for example, to make it simpler for people who want to follow those posts. So, if you were at an event, you might tweet "#JVAlert John Smith speaking on affiliate programs. Just got great idea on training affiliate managers!" Just don't get so wrapped up in tweeting that you ignore the content delivered in the conference!

7. Product or service launch. If you're about to launch a new product or introduce a new product, let your Twitter followers know, i.e. "Pre-launch pricing for new DVD set about how baby boomers can start an online biz. Get $100 early bird discount at (URL here)"

8. Responding to others with advice or answers. The way to build professional relationships on Twitter is to help your tweeps. So, if someone asks a question, comments about something to which you have a response or an idea, or you want to ask a follow-up question, this is the perfect place to do so.

9. Acknowledging new followers. I've noticed a recent trend of acknowledging people who've decided to follow a Twitter user in the past day or so. I initially thought that others were doing this as a measure of popularity, but what I've come to realize that it's actually helping out the new followers because it exposes their Twitter profiles to others who may have never heard of them and who might like to follow them. So, to thank your followers, you'd tweet, "Welcome new followers @twittername, @twittername, etc."

10. Automate your tweets. Many of my tweets have been automated and connected to other things I do. TwitterFeed turns all of my blog posts into tweets. aWeber turns each ezine issue into a tweet. EzineArticles.com tweets my followers every time I publish an article through their service. Typically all that's involved here is connecting the particular service to my Twitter account. Once all the services are connected, I get free and automated Twitter posts with no additional effort on my part.

Twitter can be a great time-waster or a wonderful way to market your business and leverage your expertise online. Follow these 10 strategies and you'll begin to attract more followers and get more clients through social networking.

About the Author

Online Business Manager and Online Business Coach Donna Gunter helps independent service professionals learn how to automate their businesses, leverage their expertise on the Internet, and get more clients online. To claim your FREE gift, TurboCharge Your Online Marketing Toolkit, visit her site at http://www.OnlineBizU.com . Follow Donna on Twitter: http://twitter.com/donnagunter

Why Twitter is a Must for Online Business?

By Walt Vieira

Oh Twitter how I love thee! Although you might not hear those exact words said very often online, you know it's true when you login to your Twitter account or visit someone's blog. With the emergence of WordPress plug-ins like "TwitThis" and the various twitter badges found on numerous blogs throughout the Internet, it is obvious people adore Twitter. Just what is it that makes this social networking site so lovable? Let's find out.

The question posed by Twitter, "What are you doing?" has become almost as popular as AOL's "You've got mail." So much so that it has even caught the eye of offline news mediums such as USA Today, CNN, and ABC. This helps to make the application popular all on its own. Those who think Twitter is just a place for computer or Internet geeks can rest assured it's nothing of the sort.

For many, Twitter is a way to interact with like-minded individuals. Whether one is a stay at home mom who craves adult conversation, an at home worker who misses the water cooler chit-chat from past jobs, or the business owner who wants to reach more of their target market, this form of social media fills a need. It makes it easier for people to connect with others in a way they might not have previously been able to.

The fact Twitter is easily accessible and even simpler to navigate makes it a favorite as well. Anyone can create a twitter account of their own with nothing more than a user name and a password. Once that's done, it's easy to customize your profile and

begin following other tweeps, as those who use Twitter affection-
ately call one another. To follow what another person is doing, just
visit their page and click the follow button. You've now been added
as a follower and when you login to your account you will see their
messages on your screen.

Want to use Twitter even when you're not at home or don't
have access to your computer? No problem. Inside your account
you can choose whether to have messages sent via cell phone or
instant messenger programs as well. Just browse to your settings
and choose the devices tab and in a few steps you're good to go.
This feature makes it possible to tweet on the go. This is perfect for
those who travel frequently or while out and about come across
something interesting or amusing that they'd like to share with
their followers.

Twitter's arrival has also lead to the creation of different
platforms and applications to make it appealing to just about
everyone. Popular applications include, Twitter Fox, Twhirl,
TweetDeck, and TweetMyBlog. Twitter Fox and Twhirl give users
who are prefer the instant messaging look and feel a way to use
Twitter in somewhat the same manner. Twitter Fox is an extension
for the Firefox browser and Twhirl is a desktop application.

TweetMyBlog is a way to automatically post updates from a
user's blog to Twitter. In order to use it all one needs is a Twitter
account and an RSS feed from their blog. It will automatically
posts a tweet using your account when your blog is updated.

Tweet Deck is another desktop application that allows for
more organization of updates. Instead of posting all a users tweets
one right after another, it allows the user to organize tweets into
separate columns within the application. For those who have
customers and friends on Twitter this is a great feature.

About the Author

Author - Walt Vieira Specialty: Internet Marketing, Mortgage and Real Estate, Author of Mortgage Secrets- 6 Steps... http://www.makemoneyfreevideo.com   http://www.rslr.net http://www.mortgagerebel.com

Twitter Tips

By Christine Imamshah

Twitter is a social networking forum where people answer the question "What Are You Doing?" in 140 characters or less. So you basically add a short note to update your friends, relatives or customers on your present activity. This article will focus on why people use Twitter and how to use it most effectively to attract traffic to your website.

Tweets, or posts to Twitter, as they are called are small updates you post that could be a thought you have had related to your business, a project you are working on, a cool video that you have watched or you could ask a question of the Twitter community. Pretty much anything goes, except for hardcore sales pitches or marketing.

One of the main reasons people come online is for interaction with others and Twitter provides a fast and easy, informal forum in which to do so.

With Twitter you follow people and they, in turn follow you which simply means that on your homepage at Twitter you will see all of the updates made by the people you are following and vice versa.

The key with any social networking is to always be adding value so please keep this in mind when you are Tweeting as well. If you do this you will tend to get a lot more followers which could mean much more traffic to your website.

You must be careful when Tweeting not to be too "salesy" as this will turn your followers off. The basic premise with Twitter and all social networking sites is interaction with others and relationship building so that they become curious and interested in what you do and visit your website.

Bear in mind that Tweets, like any other content you create online should be relevant, interesting and unique in order to generate the interest you want to drive the traffic to your website.

Twitter is free to use and can be a very handy tool for online marketers. You ought to use it and become part of the community. Especially if you work from home, Twitter and other social networking sites are a great way for you to be a part of a community which is lacking with work at home positions.

About the Author

Christine Imamshah is a full-time internet marketer. Visit my blog at http://www.christineimamshah.com and be sure to leave a comment or two. For new and excellent Traffic training head on over to http://www.explosionalmarketing.com

Give it Back to Twitter

By Daniel Massicotte

I have read several articles and podcasts on how twitter can be used for your business, to make money and guide others. The most practical uses that I have discovered is the opportunity to give back.

It's great to have a status update that tells your friends what you are up to. But don't we have Facebook for that? Why not use Twitter as a link-sharer to people who are following you.

Currently 83% of my followers are people I don't know. They found out about me on the internet through my blog or articles and decided that the kind of life I live is something they want to be exposed to more. Knowing this I tend to create Twitter updates that are not completely pointless.

Try adding a link in your Twitter. It shows that you are not just thinking about yourself. Instead you are taking your best link or discovery of the day and passing it along with the hopes that it will help someone else as it has helped you. Clearly, not following anyone on Twitter is not something completely selfish on your part. Make sure that your tweets are informative by choosing the one top highlight in the last 2 days that you were really happy to find.

I know we are just talking about Twitter, but here are some tips to keep in mind when trying to decide what to put up:

• It should be something that made you "aha!" when you first saw it.

• Mention what you found interesting in your tweet (if you have room)

• Focus on links that compliment your niche (if you have one). This will keep the people who don't know you on your list, which is more advertising power for you.

• Keep your posts light-hearted and happy.

Try to at least do that last point. John Doe from Alabama River doesn't really want to know that you had a bad day...after all, in my case that would work against the content of my site anyway!

About the Author

Dan Massicotte is perhaps the most positive oriented individual you will ever meet. You can learn more about him on his website: http://danmassicottespositiveliving.com/ Join his newsletter to be informed of new articles and website developments.

4 Easy Ways to Empower Twitter For Your Marketing Benefits

By Katie Liljeberg

Are you using Twitter to help build your online network marketing business?

If you're involved in building a business online, you know the potential that the internet can offer. It can help you attract more leads, close sales, build your brand, build your credibility in the industry, and much more. It is important to go where the traffic already is and employ several different methods to market your business; and if you're not engaging yourself in social networks, then you're terribly missing out.

One great new way to utilize social networking is through the use of Twitter Tweets. How can it help you and how do you go about using it to your advantage? Let's take a quick look at Twitter and what it has to offer.

What exactly is Twitter?

Twitter is a social networking site that allows you to network with friends, family, coworkers, and everyone else in the Twitter community. It basically helps you keep up with what people are doing at all times. You simply make a little post (called a Tweet) and everyone in the Twittersphere is now up-to-date on what is going on in your life. It is a great way to stay in touch with family and friends; but on a deeper level, it is an excellent way to see natural networking and marketing benefits.

So how can you maximize Twitter to benefit both yourself and your followers? Here are 4 easy ways to empower your Twittering for your marketing benefits:

1. Define the Outcomes You Want to Achieve

Do you want more traffic to a website? Do you want to build your image as an expert in the industry? Do you want to show your prospects who the real "you" is? Do you want to simply increase brand awareness? There are truly limitless things that you can accomplish through the use of Twitter; but your tweet activity will be more effective if you focus in on just one (or a few) objectives rather than multiple ones. Once you look at the options before you and have set your Twitter objectives, then stay disciplined with them--meaning that even though you might mix your Tweets up a bit (between personal and business), the majority of your Tweets stay on track with your main objective.

2. Provide Value to the Twittersphere & Engage in Fascinating Conversation

There are thousands of users on Twitter and it can be hard to stand out from the crowd and get noticed; so it is important to focus on providing your followers with original and useful Tweets. Engage your followers instead of just throwing out mundane details of your life. You will have more people 'replying' to you, which will in turn catch the attention of others and provide you with new followers.

Ultimately it's about adding value to the conversations that are happening on Twitter. You will become someone that people will seek out and want to interact with when you go beyond adding to the noise in the Twittersphere. Provide value, offer solutions; and remember that every Tweet counts and you are building a reputation.

3. Ask Your Followers Questions

This can create very effective Tweets and draw many followers into active conversation with you, creating a viral impact and leading to real relationships with followers.

4. Connect with as Many Twitter Users As Possible In Your Niche

"Twitter Surf" and find people in your niche that are following you and see who else they are following and the things they are Twittering about. One follower leads you to another follower and so on. To be known in your niche and build your own profile it is very important that you are interacting with others in that same niche.

Twitter can be a powerful business building tool for your online network marketing business. Stay focused on your objective, provide value, and remain active in the Twittersphere and your social networking will boost positive results.

You can see all of this in action at http://twitter.com/katielml Happy Tweeting!

Katie Liljeberg has discovered how to leverage time and technology to create a generous income from home. To learn more and to get your FREE copy of the book that takes you step-by-step and shows you how, go to: http://katielive.com/blog

Attn Ezine editors/Site owners Feel free to reprint this article in its entirety in your ezine or on your site so long as you leave all links in place, do not modify the content, and include the resource box as listed below.

About the Author

Katie Liljeberg has discovered how to leverage time and technology to create a generous income from home. To learn more and to get your FREE copy of the book that takes you step-by-step and shows you how, go to: http://katielive.com/blog

Social Media Tool Benefits: Twitter

By Matthew Bredel

Are you Twittering yet? Those new to Twitter might not really 'get' what it this social marketing tool is at first but as soon as you find some people to follow and get people following you, you're going to see the potential. Micro blogging is mini blogging and it can pack a wallop of a punch in terms of social networking and marketing because of the potential for followers who could pay attention to everything you have to say! Woo people with credit cards in their hand and you are golden!

What's interesting is how many people on the micro blogging platform are being sold something constantly and don't even realize it because they're just participating in an online discussion. Those discussions lead to links being clicked on and buzz being spread and ultimately, to people making money!

If you want to make money online and think you don't have time for a tool with 140 characters and a lot of idle chit chat, you're leaving money on the table! Look at Twitter and see all the potential.

Follow and Be Followed

Twitter only works if you're following people and they're following you. If you've joined and done nothing with your profile, it's not going to do anything for you. Follow and be followed. One doesn't work well without the other. Unless you're super famous, people won't stay on your follower list unless they feel like you're listening to them. If you're an online guru with a lot of clout people might not really care if you're on their list because they still want to know what you're saying but if you're going to use the tool, you need to be prepared to converse with the little people and avoid elitism. That's not to say you have to follow every single person that clicks on your name, though. There's a fair bit of Twitter spam going on so you'll want to be a little bit choosy about whether you follow someone or not. And, that tells you right there what you shouldn't use Twitter for. Spammers quickly get ignored with this tool.

Twitter Tools

Because Twitter is a pretty basic tool, there are a lot of advantages to using some of the free tools that exist to enhance the Twitter experience. There are dozens of tools that help you get Twitter doing what you want or help you mine the user base for information. Tools like Tweetdeck, Twhirl, TwitterFox, Tweet-Beep, Hashtags, Twittermail, Twitterly and more all have varying features and benefits that can help you maximize the earning potential.

Success from Reciprocity

Reciprocity is key to success on this social marketing tool. Because it's a virtual water cooler environment, you need to be a positive contributor in order to gain benefits from it. After you find a group to follow and get some people to follow you, you need to converse, you need to provide value and you should establish yourself as a valuable person to follow. Then, people will do things like: click your URL, re-tweet your interesting tweets, tell others to follow you, write @before your username so their followers can see you might be worth following, social bookmarking your interesting tweets, digging your URLs and more. See how this tool can help you?

About the Author

Are you interested in making money with Twitter? Learn more social marketing potential and about making money with Twitter at Tru-Social-Guru and TheWebReviewer.

My Top 7 Essential Twitter Tools

By Donna Gunter

Unless you've been hiding under a rock, you have probably heard something about the new micro blogging platform, Twitter, and how Twitter has taken the online marketing world by storm. The phenomenon has even spawned a new lingo, with new your new tweeps (followers) tweeting (making posts) you and discussing the state of the Twitterverse (you get the idea here).

While Twitter is pretty easy to use, there's an overwhelming amount of tools, plug-ins and applications being developed to support it. I ran across one blog that listed over 100. How can you determine which ones will best support you in your use of Twitter?

I've tried to sort through all of the junk, and come up with my 7 essential Twitter tools:

1. TwitterFox. This is actually a Firefox browser plug-in that permits you to keep up with your tweets and any direct (private) messages that come your way. Tweetdeck and Twhirl similarly help your manage your tweets and tweeps and have gotten rave reviews from users, but I prefer the simplicity of Twitterfox. All I have to do is check the Twitter logo in the lower right corner of any browser window to check my Tweets and to reply to any of them that I want.

2. TweetLater. The primary function of TweetLater.com is to permit die-hard Twitterers to stock up Tweets that can be

scheduled to be posted over a period of time. However, the reason that I like it is that I can forward the emails about who is following me to my TweetLater email address, and my will automatically get a direct message from me. I just love it when I can automate my marketing tasks!

3. TwitterFeed. This service will enable you to feed your blog posts to your Twitter account. You can control the frequency with which Twitter displays your blog post, as well as the text used to preface your blog feed. I use "Blog update" to preface my posts.

4. TwitterSearch. This site offers a quick way to search what people are posting about particular topics or keywords in the twitterverse.

5. TweetBeep. This is the equivalent of Google Alerts for Twitter, which permits you to track mentions of your name, products, company, or anything else you want to track.

6. LoudTwitter. LoudTwitter is the bridge that posts your daily Tweets to your blog Your blog takes care about the archiving of your tweets along with your other posts, which give more context. After all, if you have a blog and a Twitter, your blog is probably the core place where you want to be found and tracked.

7. Png.fm. While technically not a Twitter tool, I quickly tired of manually updating my status settings at all of my social networking sites. So, I began using Ping.fm. When you update your status at Ping.fm, the service will automatically update your status on all of your social networking sites, like Twitter, Face-book, Plurk, Pownce, to name a few (there are 21 you can update). Depending on the number of networks you use, it will take you 10-50 minutes to connect your Ping.fm account to your various social network accounts. However, once everything is set up, you simply log into your Ping account, post your update (no more than 140 characters), and your status is automatically upgraded on all of your social networking profiles. I use this tool to post Tweets, but use Twitterfox to post my @ replies to my followers.

Even though Twitter initially seemed like a fad, it's not going away. Use these tools to maximize your use of Twitter and enhance your social networking!

About the Author

Online Business Manager and Online Business Coach Donna Gunter helps independent service professionals learn how to automate their businesses, leverage their expertise on the Internet, and get more clients online. To claim your FREE gift, TurboCharge Your Online Marketing Toolkit, visit her site at http://www.OnlineBizU.com . Follow Donna on Twitter: http://twitter.com/donnagunter

Does Twitter Have Any SEO Value?

By Seybold Scientific

This question came to Seybold Scientific via Twitter last night about the value of using Twitter as a part of your SEO strategy. Twitter is a great social networking tool to create relationships with your 'followers' about the activities of your business. From a structural standpoint, Twitter creates a "nofollow" tag advising Search Engines to ignore all posted links. While it is not primarily an influential SEO tool, it is an invaluable SMO (Social Media Optimization) tool. Twitter and other social media tools, like Twitter, are primarily extensions for your branding and awareness strategy, which will allow you to manage your credibility as a source for influencing the generation of SEO opportunities. From a traffic perspective, many bloggers and businesses are using Twitter as an incremental source of traffic and link juice with varying degrees of success. Twitter's primary benefit is the ability to create a viral marketing tool delivered to a willing audience. Take, as an example, @ricksanchezcnn. In July Rick Sanchez of CNN began to use Twitter as a means to communicate with and market to his viewers. As a result he has claimed to have seen a rise in his ratings as a result of the interactivity between himself and his viewers via Twitter. Rick Sanchez has been able to convert his Twitter activity to an increased audience. If you follow Mr. Sanchez, you will notice that his posts are not just questions about news items. Often times you will find him posting about his family time, or impressions of something he just saw on TV. Social Media tools allow you to put a personality behind your brand, learn more about your customers through interaction. When thinking about Twitter as a source of traffic, think about how your personality builds the type of goodwill and awareness into business. It is telling how the further we stray from the corner store, Social Media has inserted those concepts and values that made the corner store the engine that drove our commercial decisions. In short, Twitter is not an SEO tool. Twitter is one of the great online PR and marketing tools that can be used to build your brand and client base through "word of mouth" and personality. More information available at Seybold Scientific

About the Author

Seybold Scientific is a performance-based digital marketing and SEO company offering a range of services from initial consultancy, design services, organic and paid search marketing to fully-managed online marketing campaigns to optimize your return on online investment.

Twitter: Not A Waste Of Time For Small Business Owners

By Jennifer Haubein

Social networking has changed the way we do business and the biggest change has been for small business owners.

Small businesses usually have one person who makes a great representative for the company in the social networking arena. And this makes small businesses a perfect fit for a social networking tool called Twitter.

Twitter is a micro-blogging tool in which you have 140 characters to answer the question "What Are You Doing?"

At first I was reluctant to join in on Twitter and wanted to make sure I would see business results from it. Since connecting through Twitter I have seen these results: more Website and Blog traffic; product ideas from my target market; and an increase in expert status. Another bonus, Twitter makes working from home not so isolating and I feel as if I'm in an office talking around the water cooler.

So how can you obtain these results for your business?

1. Create a Compelling Twitter Profile - Add a professional photo to your Twitter profile, because no one will follow you without a photo. Include a link to your main website and create an interesting bio that entices people to find out more.

2. Create Interesting and Useful Tweets (a Twitter message) - Don't just write about your personal life, but also include blog

posts, links to articles and anything else your target market would be interested in.

3. Follow Others - Start off by following others in Twitter and return the follow when they follow you.

4. Automate It - Use your cell phone with Twitter and update your status while you're on the run. Within Twitter click on the settings tab and then the devices tab. Within this section you will be able to add your and setup your cell phone to work with Twitter. Also, I have my blog set up to automatically post new posts to Twitter. This is a great time saver and generates a lot more traffic to my blog.

5. Is Your Target Market on Twitter? Before jumping in on Twitter I would consider if your target market is there yet. If you target small business owners then, yes, Twitter will work great for you. Also the younger generation is very involved in Twitter. So think about your target market and where they are.

Action Step: Create a Twitter profile at Twitter.com and you can start off by following me @jhaubein. I look forward to connecting with you.

About the Author

Jennifer Haubein publishes "SiteNotes" a FREE bi-weekly ezine for small business owners who want a website that actually works. If you're ready to get insider tips website developers don't want you to know, and start making more money online, get your FREE tips now at http://www.BestBizWebsiteSolutions.com/newsletter.html.

Skyrocketing Your Business With Twitter

By Scott Brooks

Twitter was established in 2006 and since has become one of the most successful instant messaging websites online. It is essentially a social networking website that allows friends, family members, colleagues and customers to keep up with other individuals are businesses. Twitter was created to allow people to stay connected with acquaintances, family and friends. User's updates where to answer the question "What are you doing?" Twitter provides a platform for individuals to update others about their daily lives. Twitter can also be used in a very effective way for marketers and companies.

This site can be used as an extremely simply way to update one's customers about what is going on in their business, to notify one's customers about upcoming sales, specials and discounts. Marketers would be wise to encourage their customers to sign up for Twitter by offering some type of special sales prices or exclusive sales notices for those who sign up to follow them. Having special sales and providing "insider" announcements for this group is a good way to take advantage of the medium.

Twitter can also be used as a great customer service tool. Marketers can ask questions about their customer's take on their products, service or support. They can answer and address any complaints as well.

Twitter is also an inexpensive and fast way for marketers to stay in touch with their customers. They can do so instantly at no cost. Unlike email blasts which require a special type of software or company that manages messages that are sent out, Twitter only takes a few minutes. A company's or marketer's list can instantly be contacted in a very short amount of time.

Internet users love social networking websites. It gives them an opportunity to feel a part of a community. It also allows them to get important information on their own time and when they decide to. Unlike email marketing, which can easily begin to bug customers, can be filtered and sometimes are even ignored, if someone is checking in on your twitter updates, they are actually interested in what is going on with your company. As a result, you have a captive, loyal audience that is more likely to buy from you.

Twitter should be monetized. However, avoid trying to sell some type of product every time you send out an update. If you do, you will quickly turn people off. Instead, provide them with well thought out and helpful posts. Only send out sales pitches occasionally and then only about products that you are familiar with and would recommend to your family or friends. Your goal is to use Twitter as a long term tool. If you begin constantly pushing products, you will alienate your readers.

About the Author

Need a quick and easy solution for driving targeted traffic to you website? Go here: http://www.downloadsuniverse.com

Scott Brooks is a successful internet marketer who has been working online since 2004. He has authored several popular eBooks and owns three membership sites.

5 Best Twitter Marketing Ideas

By Guy Siverson

In my last article I looked at How To Use Twitter To Promote Your Blog Or Website, which focused on linking article directories to your Twitter profile

In this article I'd like to review 5 best Twitter marketing ideas. This information was compiled as a result of an article I read on ProBlogger.

*** BE CONSISTENT ***

You have to be serious about your project before people will really take you seriously. I make it a personal goal to write 2 articles every day. One I post to my blog while I pst the other to my website. I've been doing this for about 2 months now. Over time people will see how serious I am about building SEO & Beyond and as a result my audience popularity will grow. However, this doesn't apply just to me or just to Internet Marketing focus. This fact will be true for anyone who is attempting to build an audience for any niche market.

*** BE ORIGINAL & USEFUL ***

Remember the essay tests in school? You knew that if you wrote enough to make it look like you know what you were talking about there was a good chance you would get a good essay grade based on content alone.

Such is not the case here. If a person takes the time to read your article only to find... * No helpful ideas * No take away content * No unique ideas

You can practically guarantee one major fact as being true. * No future reader of your other articles.

Therefore, if you don't have something to say; you'll be more respected in the long run if you simply don't pretend that you do.

*** ASK THE EXPERTS ***

My niche topic is Internet Marketing. I have become an SEO & Bum Marketing expert in my own right. I know some about other areas too, such as the one that I'm writing on today. However, to say that I am a Twitter Expert or Social Networking specialist would be anything but the case. I'm learning, but I'm not afraid to ask the experts in these areas for their advice. Fact is I am creating a place on my website where experts can share their expertise with an exclusive article for their information. It's yet to catch on so far, but considering my website is only 4 months old at time of this writing I'm more than willing to give it time.

*** SHARE ***

Sure you want to post all your articles to Twitter. Why not. However, how do you think it looks for you to be the only poster in your profile? Kin to talking to a wall perhaps? That's why it's a great idea to share articles and ideas of others in your industry over your Twitter account.

*** WRAP UP *** * Be consistent * Be useful * Be original * Be open * Be informative

And you will be well on your way to excellent twitter marketing.

About the Author

Guy Siverson (AKA SEOGuy) If you liked this article read How To Use Twitter To Promote Your Blog @ http://www.viralmarketing4u.com/2008/09/how-to-use-twitter-to-promote-your-blog.html. - Partner of http://Search-Engine-Optimization-And-Beyond.com

How To Use Twitter To Promote Your Blog

By Guy Siverson

Twitter.

Yet another Social Networking WEB 2.0 tool for you to use to promote your blog or website. I just finished a YouTube video that told how to make comments on Twitter as well as add a side widget to watch comments that others are making. Both ideas are really good advice.

Here's how to use Twitter to promote your blog by writing articles.

Assuming that you have already written your article (my favorite method is bum marketing) and posted your article to your blog or website in this article we look at what to do with it next.

*** SETUP TWITTER ***

If you are going to use Twitter.com you need to set it up. This includes creating an account, completing your profile and setting up all the settings to your preferences. Be sure to include a relevant picture to your campaign purposes.

My own personal Twitter handle is SEOGuy2. If you are interested in topics related to Internet Marketing I encourage you to join my community.

*** ARTICLE DIRECTORIES ***

With your article in hand and twitter profile setup it's time to "feed the bird". I personally use EzineArticles.com for this part of the process. Which means the next step is for you to create an account with Ezine Articles.

Many people make the mistake of creating an account, adding it to their automated article submission tool & considering it a job well done. In my opinion it is a job half done. I'm not against automated article submission services to be sure, but they do tend to encourage people to miss the greater advantages of article directories like Ezine Articles.

*** CREATE A PROFILE ***

Are you aware that many article directories allow you to create a profile on their service? It's true. But Ezine Articles does one better than that, which is why I their article directory is in my top 10 list.

Okay, with your account created navigate to your personal bio under the profile manager. Here you are able to add your URL's to various areas including Twitter.

Here's the best part. "If you have a Twitter account, we can automatically update your status when your articles are approved."

Which means that as you write and the articles are posted on EzineArticles they are automatically posted to Twitter at the exact same time. I call that a 2 for one process which is easy to setup.

I also call it the best how to use twitter to promote your blog or website process that I know of. Like I said, there are others. But this is the best as it is a completely hands free process that is available for all to use.

About the Author

Guy Siverson (AKA SEOGuy) - If you liked this article read 5 Best Twitter Marketing Ideas @ http://SEO-and-beyond.com/A-Art-Dir/Tit1/Using-Blogs-And-Forums-Correctly/5-Best-Twitter-Marketing-Ideas.htm. - Partner of http://ViralMarketing4u.com

List Building: 7 Steps to Grow Your Email List with Twitter

By Donna Gunter

Twitter is a micro blogging platform that has taken the business world by storm, 140 characters per post. The purpose of Twitter is to post short updates (not to exceed 140 characters) about what you're doing at the moment, read the updates of others whom you're following (in a non-stalker way), and comment and reply on what they're doing.

All kinds of applications have been developed for Twitter, and I've discovered that people either love to tweet (i.e. submit a Twitter post) or the whole concept drives them crazy. I admit that seeing all the tweets exchanged among those I follow can be overwhelming (like being in a big instant message universe where everyone can see everyone else's messages), but I am having success in getting to know my fellow Twitter peeps and in getting the word out about my business and in growing my list.

As I became accustomed to tweeting daily, I began to wonder if I was missing a key business marketing strategy in the process, and then a colleague told me about her strategy of sending a direct message, or DM (this is a private message goes directly to your Twitter pal via email and can't be seen by others) thanking them for following her, as well as a short introduction to her business. I thought that was a wonderful idea, began to implement that strategy, and saw results immediately.

Then I read a great post by Denise Wakeman of The Blog Squad on building your list with Twitter, and knew I had to incorporate this idea into my marketing strategy. Here's the steps I took to maximize my use of Twitter to grow my email list:

1. Create a Twitter account. Your Twitter ID can be your given name, or you may want to use your Twitter ID to brand yourself, i.e. Organizing Queen. Just get the basics set up at this point. In the setup, check both options of "Email when someone starts following me" as well as "Email when I receive a new direct message."

2. Have a freebie to give away. You may want to create a unique electronic giveaway just for your Twitter followers, or you can use the same giveaway that you already use on your site. Once you've decided what to give away, create a squeeze page and insert sales copy and an opt-in form so that you can direct your Twitter followers to this page for them to join your list and receive your free giveaway. For tracking purposes, you may want to set up a unique page to see just how many subscribers join your list from this invitation.

3. Twitter bio: You have 160 characters to describe your business as a part of your Twitter bio. Describe yourself and your call to action. Here's a sample: "Houston Professional Organizer. Follow me for free eBook to learn how to clear your clutter in 30 days."

4. Set up TweetLater.com account and welcome message: The aspect of this service that you'll be using is the ability to send an automatic message to new followers, which you should turn on as a part of setting up your account. You can choose a public or direct (private) message. Choose to send the private message. This message is limited to 140 characters, as it's a tweet, so here's a sample along the same lines as the sample mentioned earlier: "Thx 4 following. Get free eBook to help clear clutter in 30 days @ <your website squeezepage URL here>." I have also turned on the ability to automatically follow new followers.

6. Twitter email address. When you create your Twitter account, use an email address that is attached to an account or software that will enable you to forward all new follower notifications that you get from Twitter. My email software doesn't offer that forwarding capability, so I changed my Twitter email address to my Gmail address, and used the filter capability to create a Twitter label and to forward all of my follower notifications to my TweetLater.com account.

As a part of the account setup, TweetLater gives you the email address to which you forward those notifications as well as instructions on setting up your rules for your email forwarding. What happens when this is set up correctly is that anytime anyone decides to follow you in Twitter, they automatically get your direct email message to join your list without you having to do anything.

If needed, be sure and update your email address in your TweetLater account. You can also forward these messages manually to your TweetLater email address and achieve the same purpose. In order for this to work, the email address in your TweetLater account must match the email address in your Twitter account.

7. Test your setup. To ensure that this setup was working for me, I set up a "fake" Twitter account just for testing, using one of my free account email addresses. In my "fake" account, I found my "real" Twitter profile and clicked "Follow". Within minutes I got an email message that my "fake" account is following my "real" account, and then at my "fake" account email address, I received my TweetLater direct mail message about getting my free eBook, and a second email that my "real" account is following my "fake" account.

Twitter is a wonderful tool to help you add your Twitter followers to your list, which is one way you can create deeper relationships with your target market to help them get to know, like, and trust you. Start Twittering today and begin to experience amazing list growth!

About the Author

Online Business Manager and Online Business Coach Donna Gunter helps independent service professionals learn how to automate their businesses, leverage their expertise on the Internet, and get more clients online. To claim your FREE gift, TurboCharge Your Online Marketing Toolkit, visit her site at http://www.OnlineBizU.com . Ask Donna an Internet Marketing question at http://www.AskDonnaGunter.com

Free Download: "The Twitter Report" - Twitter Marketing

By Arneard Wilks Jr

Twitter is a fast growing "micro-blogging" service and social network all wrapped into one. After some bumpy roads & strong growing pains the free service that allows hyper-connectedness & an interesting way to express "what you're doing" at any given time, seems to be on the fast track now to becoming the next mega success story online.

Twitter was founded by Evan Williams, who is no rookie to bringing creative ideas to multi-million dollar reality. Evan was a blogging pioneer and has created & grown web properties that have attracted the attention of the big dogs, including Google.

One of Evan's past web projects grew to be so huge, in fact, that Google bought him out for a multimillion dollar price tag.

Rather than reclining on a beach chair & sipping Coronas for the remainder of his life, Evan decided to try his hand again, when he thought up the concept of "micro-blogging."

In all our modern day internet hustle & bustle there's come a need for brevity... short, to the point, yet meaningful messages.

Evan's idea for Twitter was a service that not only allows people to post short "micro-blog" entries (by enforcing a self-created parameter that only allows users a maximum of 140 characters per post), but also helps people stay connected through the use of followers, text messages, and @replies.

The Twitter faithful are even coining their own new lingo to describe some of the everyday actions that take place on the site. "Tweets," for example, are the term used to describe each of your short, 140 character or less, posts to update your Twitter profile.

In this article the aim is to go over a simple overview of the everyday things you'll need to know in order to get started on Twitter & set yourself up for maximum exposure using this free service.

First off, you'll need to go create an account by visiting the site and following the easy to follow prompts for creating a new account.

Once you're all setup, be sure to visit the "Settings" tab and customize your profile and also enter a short bio, along with the URL to your website.

In order to double the chances of getting a click, I'd also recommend including a hyperlink within your bio, in addition to the hyperlink you'll enter in the box for your web URL.

The next thing you'll want to do is visit the "Devices" tab and get your account setup so that you can send tweets on the go from your mobile phone.

The steps for confirming your mobile device to work with Twitter are easy to follow and you'll be up and rolling in no time flat.

Once you've got your new account created and have configured your settings & mobile, it's time to start tweeting.

Remember, you'll be limited to 140 characters per message so choose your words wisely. If you'd like to include a hyperlink with your Tweet you should consider shortening it down using a free tool like Tiny URL, or Snip URL.

Be careful not to come off as too spammy by including links in every Tweet... get involved with the Twitter community and share some of your daily activities with your followers so you can get a real feel for what it's all about before sucking traffic out... it's got to be a give-give relationship!

Now, to really get yourself on the fast track and start adding new followers fast, the best advice is to follow people who you find interesting, and single out those who already have a large followership. Tweet regularly and often using your mobile, the Twitter site, and even handy third party applications like "Twhirl."

Anytime you see a new Tweet from someone you are following send them an @reply by including the "@" sign + their Twitter username in a message responding to their original tweet.

By sending users an @reply you'll get their attention, strike up conversations, and best of all - put yourself in the public spotlight so that all of their followers will take notice of you.

Before you know it, you'll be addicted to Twitter and will have a massive followership as well!

Once you've built a followership it's easy to get visitors to your site by using services like TwitterFeed anytime you post a new blog entry, TweetLater to automatically direct message new followers, and other little known tips & tricks for putting it all on auto-pilot.

Twitter is a new revolution in communications and may be the first glimpse at Web 3.0. I recommend getting setup on Twitter today so you can ride this new wave into the future and enjoy it for all it's worth!

About the Author

-- To learn how you can get more targeted free traffic from Twitter on auto-pilot, visit: http://www.linkbrander.com/go/67776

How to Use Twitter to Connect With Customers

By Jon Davis

The "micro-blogging" service Twitter has become more mainstream since the company's inception in 2006. Twitter users now number well into the millions, with no signs of slowing growth. While Twitter is most popular on the West Coast, users are spreading rapidly throughout the world. Companies are finding many creative ways to use Twitter to benefit their businesses: to run promotions, provide high-quality customer service, get product feedback, manage their brands and perform market research.

Promotions
Many companies are using Twitter as a means of rolling out cheap but effective promotions. One such company, Whole Foods Market, is using Twitter heavily to connect with customers.

Whole Foods Twitter account has become a valuable way for the company to market specific products and boost store sales. Whole Foods runs a weekly Twitter promotion where they "Tweet" (or send) a pass phrase and a specific store location; the first 5 people who go to that location and give the password receive a $25 store gift. Another way to earn a $25 gift certificate is the "Tweet of the Day". Whole Foods monitors all of the Tweets about them using the Twitter search tool. Each day, the Tweet that was particularly funny or interesting wins the prize, with the Twitter user receiving a direct message alerting them that they have won. At this time Whole Foods has more than 2,900 followers on Twitter.

I believe that Twitter is a great place for larger companies to market their products and interact with customers because their customers are actively seeking it. Whole Foodsthousands of followers have made the conscious decision to follow Whole Foods on Twitter. They want to know what is going on and what is new at Whole Foods. It's like signing up for an e-mail newsletter, but people are more apt to simply follow someone on Twitter because it doesn't fill up their inbox. And if they have a question, they can get a personal response as opposed to a stale e-mail reply. Personally, during a recent salmonella poisoning scare in Georgia, I direct-messaged Whole Foods and asked what they were doing to help protect against the problem in their stores. I received a direct response three hours later. What a great customer service experience! They provided exactly the information I was looking for and displayed the power of reaching out to customers.

Customer Service

Many businesses are adopting Twitter as a means of providing customer service. On the flip side, consumers are finding that, often, Twitter is the best way to communicate with large companies whose customer service tends to lack at times.

Comcast, for instance, is having success using Twitter to better address their customers concerns and issues. The most famous situation involves Comcast and TechCrunch blogger Michael Arrington. Frustrated that his service had been out for hours, Arrington eventually lost his cool and began angrily Twittering his frustrations. Within 20 minutes he was contacted by a Twitter executive and his problem was resolved. It is true that Arrington is an influential person and this could have helped his cause, but every day Comcast is helping plenty of lesser-known customers, as well. Comcast reports that they receive millions of calls a day from customers looking for help. Conversely, the 10-member Comcast team that manages Twitter and other social networks helps about 100 customers a day. Consequently, the Comcast reps managing their Twitter account are able to address the problem better and give a quick solution.

Other large companies are also using Twitter to addressing customer service issues, including Southwest Air, Home Depot and Dell. Are your customers on Twitter? If you operate on the West Coast, the chances are yes. If not or if you don't know, go to the Twitter search tool and type in your companies name and products. Maybe some potential customers are out there. Try searching for some of the services you provide. If you find some people out in the Twitter universe talking about your company or services, join the conversation and just watch how much they appreciate the personal contact.

Brand Management and Market Research
What if finding out what your customers are saying about your service or product was as easy as typing in your company name or product into a search bar? Once you searched, you were met with real customers talking in real time about your company and products. With Twitter, this is possible.

Using the search tool, you can search all the Tweets made by every user in the Twitter network in real time. This can be a powerful way for your company to leverage your brand online. Imagine rolling out a new product and seeing in real time how it is being received by the public. You can see what they are saying. If your customers are having any problems, you will know right away and can send them a message as to how best solve their issues. You can even set up a personalized system to alert you via e-mail if someone Tweets about your company using Tweet Scan.

Want to find out what people are saying about the competition? Use the same search tools to type in your competitors names and see if there might be something you could use to your advantage. Find out what people like or don't like about their products or services. Discover what their customers really like and consider implementing it yourself.

Even if you can't find someone talking about your company or services today, they likely will be in the future. Your company needs to be prepared for the day when Twitter is used even more widely. I would strongly encourage you to go to Twitter and at least sign-up your company with a handle (Twitter account name) that will protect your brand in the future. When creating your account, you can even modify your account page to have the same feel and color scheme as your website. You wouldn't want someone to use your company's name as their handle and spread bad or unauthorized information as Twitter grows.

Jon Davis is an Internet marketing analyst with Capture Commerce, an organic SEO company in the metro Atlanta area.

About the Author

Jon Davis is an Internet marketing analyst with Capture Commerce, an organic SEO company in the metro Atlanta area.

Twitter and Facebook -- The Art and Science of Efficient Communication

By Pandit Sumit

Although Twitter is great for people of all walks of life and professions, it is probably best for what it was designed for originally: keeping in touch with friends. Twitter makes keeping in touch with friends easier and simpler than ever before.

Because you can tweet, or update, so many different ways, it's flexible enough to be used from anywhere, which lends itself to being used more frequently than sites like MySpace or Facebook.

Keeping in touch with friends on MySpace/Facebook can sometimes be a challenge because you have so much other noise from people and things you may not care about. Maybe you have a handful of people that post the same bulletins frequently and they clutter up your bulletin board or mini-feed and you sometimes miss a bulletin that your close friends post. Twitter eliminates all of this because there is inherently less noise, and all tweets are limited to 140 characters or less.

There are no friends requests, event invitations, application requests or any of the other distractions you can find on MySpace/Facebook, there is only the status update. The status update is really all that's important when it comes to keeping up with friends because it allows you to see at a glance what a bunch of your friends are up to.

Twitter detaches the status update from your computer and even your web browser. Users can tweet via text message, desktop Twitter clients and IM. This allows for a social network with more flexibility than most others. Sure, Facebook has a great mobile iPhone version, but not everyone has an iPhone or even a phone with a web browser.

Updating Twitter via text message is something that anyone with any phone can do and that is why it is better than MySpace/Facebook for keeping in touch with friends.

But what are some of the ways that friends can use Twitter to communicate more frequently and make a tangible difference in their lives?

Making Plans via Twitter Twitter makes making plans simple and fast. Once your core group of friends that you hang out with regularly is using Twitter, you might find that you're all hanging out even more because now everyone knows what's going on for the next outing.

Now if you're trying to get everyone together for the midnight premiere of Indiana Jones, you don't have to call each person individually and then negotiate the time to meet up and the theater to watch it at. All you have to do is post something along the lines of "Whose down to see Indy tonight at midnight in Alhambra?"

As long as everyone checks Twitter at some point during the day, everyone will reply saying yes, no or suggesting other plans. Bam! Plans suggested and made within minutes with one 140 character message on your part. Beautiful.

Announcing Good News Now when something good happens, it's easier to spread the word. Let's say you just got promoted, maybe you wouldn't bother to call your 10 closest friends to brag, but that doesn't mean that they wouldn't be happy for you and glad to hear about it. Twitter makes it easy to get a virtual round of high fives within minutes of announcing your good news.

Sharing Photo Album Links How many times have you gone to an event where one of your friends is taking pictures all night? It sure would be nice to get those pictures, but somehow it rarely ever gets done. It's only when you had an exceptionally great trip or fun time that you get to see your friend's pictures. Now it's easy to post a link to a zip file uploaded to zShare and then share it with your friends through Twitter. Just upload it and post the link for everyone to see.

Get their attention by using @replies and you've just sent it to them in a hurry and they can all download the zip file and then talk about the pictures and the good times.

Sharing Regular Links Sharing links to new web sites, music or videos is also made more efficient now, thanks to Twitter. Gone are the days of IMing everyone with some new viral video. Now all you have to do is Twitter it and all your friends, who likely have the same taste as you anyway, will now see that you think they should check out this new find.

Chances are, you don't tell everyone you know about every cool thing you find on the internet, but that doesn't mean that they wouldn't be interested if you let them know. It's the same idea as using it to spread good news. Just because you don't want to take the time to tell them, doesn't mean they wouldn't like to hear about it.

I hope you now see some ways to use Twitter that you hadn't thought about before. At its best, Twitter can really help bring people closer together and I hope this post can bring you closer to those you care about.

Speaking of bringing people closer together, you should follow me on Twitter! If you have some other friend-related uses for Twitter, please post them in the comments.

About the Author

For more useful tips and hints, please browse for more information at our website:- www.blog-and-ping.com www.blogging.reprintarticlesite.com

Find out more about Web 2.0 - Flickr, Twitter, del.icio.us etc

By Amandeep Singh

The Internet is alive with places to market your business, and more are coming on the scene each day. This can lead to hyperactive attempts to conduct comprehensive internet marketing 2.0 campaigns, but it is not always worth leaping onto each new bandwagon. Particularly if you have a limited budget.

However, some sites are leading the way in their field and do provide valuable opportunities for Online Public Relations (PR) and marketing at very little expense.

Social Bookmarks Del.icio.us led the way back in 2003, offering every Internet user the chance to bookmark sites and content of interest at del.icio.us and share those with other users. Delicious has grown from strength to strength and offers websites a valuable chance to gain back links and exposure. Others in a similar vein are Digg, Furl, Reddit, and Stumbleupon. You can easily access this audience by adding the appropriate code into the footer of your site, or after valuable content or articles, so that your visitor adds you to their list of social bookmarks.

Photo Galleries Flickr was one of the first sites that offered users the chance to share their photos with the rest of the world. It is worth creating a photo album of your company's products and photos, and where permissible allowing these photos to be used on other peoples websites, with an accreditation, particularly if the photo clearly shows your brand, logo, URL etc.

Twitter Once upon a time there was blogging, and now there is twitter. This is a seemingly meaningless application that allows users to send messages from their mobile phone or through a Web application on to the Twitter website (or your own) to say, What I am doing now. Twitter could prove to be one of those social networking experiences which may die out over time, or it could become part of your marketing toolbox.

For canny marketers however Twitter is being used as a tool which offers a very simple method to regularly inform customers about products, services etc, and to widen exposure of your company. Whether you twitter during the launch of a product, or twitter whilst at an exhibition, conference or awards ceremony, or use it as a mini-blog, or to announce a sale of your products, you can use this tool effectively to capture the interest of your customers and promote what you are doing with your business. A Senior Manager at Amazon uses it, and if he does, you can be sure that Amazon are finding value in it as a communication and marketing tool.

Whichever of the new social tools you decide to incorporate into your marketing strategy, you should ensure that they build on your current policies and fit your budget, and particularly the time available to you. A blog or twitter site that is full of enthusiasm one day and then abandoned the next does nothing for the image of your company.

About the Author

Did you find this article useful? For more useful tips & hints, Points to ponder and keep in mind, techniques & insights pertaining to Google Ad sense, Do please browse for more information at our website :-

http://www.seo-prediction.com
http://www.seo.reprintarticlesite.com

Twitter is building a nest for my Networking Business

By World Wide Weller

Twitter is definitely chirping quite a buzz. Now a standard on every profile I have listed with my social media web 2.0 sites. Time to turn off the phone, shut down the email, and tweet to be left alone. Where's World Wide Weller...What does his nest say? Twitter gives you a fragmented experience of opinions, events, news, ideas and feedback largely because its structured to accommodate non-contextual usability:

You can easily follow thousands of users and listen in and enter into conversations conducted among multiple users at any point. Now here comes the articles for twitter etiquette, you know the people that twitter more than 20 times a day, or broadcasting absolutely nothing relevant to their actual twitter moment.

It sure has been an entertaining media for the big hitters in the online marketing and network marketing arena to quickly chirp back and forth at each other. Us followers find it quite amusing. I twitter more business oriented informational moments. Nothing more exciting than receiving a Twitter email saying I have a new follower.

I am the most entertaining twitterer of them all...late night to see if I can get any twittering responses. Come follow me for a twitter extravaganza www.twitter.com/WorldWideWeller

Welcome to Prosperity, Michael www.IAmANetworkMarketer.com

About the Author

World Wide Weller is taking Online and Network Marketing to a whole new level with the most aggressive dynamic online marketing system with a fully customizable self branding approach that is duplicated as well as extensive training.

Internet Ministry: I Like Twitter and You Will Too!

By Bishop James I Feel God Brown

Internet Ministry: I Like Twitter and You Will Too!

Ministry is about providing service for the glory of God. In order to provide that service. We communicate with people with the objective of letting them see God's glory within us. So effective ministry, always involves communication with people.

Internet ministry, at its root, is also about communication! Because the technology of the Internet allows us greater access to a huge number of people, it is a great medium to expand the Kingdom of God.

With the advent of Web 2.0 technology, social networking, blogging, as well as, teleconferencing, we may feel overwhelmed about what systems to use in order to communicate with people for the Kingdom. I don't mean to suggest that every time we speak to someone, it should be about salvation. However, no one will care about salvation, until they know that we are real people who care about them.

We are now communicating with people that we otherwise would not have access to in the past. However, because of various problems with e-mail communications, instant messaging, and privacy, these same people are becoming more difficult to reach.

Since I spend large amounts of my day on line, I'm very cautious about jumping on board with new platforms.

But, recently I found a platform that really worked for purposes that I had never consciously intended.

Over the last few months there's been a lot of buzz about twitter. Twitter me this, and twitter me that. Nonetheless, I was not all a twit over twitter. After all, I already had a MySpace page. My face was on Facebook. I was tubing on YouTube, and I even had a few friends who had developed networks using NING.

So the last thing I wanted was another social networking tool. Especially one that would allow people to see what I was doing every day all day. I didn't believe I needed another distraction. I was already behind enough already.

But when I started using twitter, I was pleasantly surprised at how much I enjoyed it. Three things impressed me about twitter. 1. I could easily find and access others that were doing Internet ministry (or any niche), and who I could learn from and share with, in the process. 2. I found highly involved people on twitter and was able to carry on conversations, even though they would never have even answered my e-mail, otherwise. 3. I found information that was still in the planning stages and seminars I was unaware of. This allowed me to be prepared, strategically, to better serve my mission and objectives.

In my mind twitter has been more effective in helping me promote Internet ministry than any of the other social networks. It is so much simpler to use than MySpace, so much more responsive than Facebook, so much more interactive than LinkedIn.

In other words, I just like it! I think you will too!

FYI my twitter page is http://twitter.com/ifeelgod - Come Follow there!

For more information on using technology in ministry visit http://fromchurch.com

About the Author

Bishop James Brown aka "I Feel God" is the founder or the http://1000churches.org network and he is called "The Internet's Favorite Pastor". In addition, Bishop is a prolific writer and speaker who is in demand for his insights. You can read his daily Blog at http://ifeelgod.org and find information on using the Internet for ministry at http://fromchurch.com

How To Get To Know Twitter & Your Fellow Tweeps

By Amy Cacher

If you find yourself in a position that you need to understand your target customer as well as keep up with various ways of marketing to those potential customers, Twitter is one of the most powerful and popular tools out there right now! This new type of network communication has been taken up by companies and individuals alike in recent months and for good reason.

To get a better understanding of Twitter, let's first take a look at the format. Essentially, Twitter is a program that allows you to make very small, public posts. Because these posts are so limited (they max out at 140 characters) they can easily be sent to a number of different locations all at once. When you have written a Twitter, it can appear on the twitter website, on short message services, instant messaging sites or even on third-party applications like Facebook or Twitterific. Folks can even add a script to their blog or website to show their most recent posts and the posts of others! Your Twitter messages, also known tweets, will appear to anyone who has chosen to follow your updates.

There are several advantages to this type of communication. The first thing that you will discover is that it allows for a much more immediate relay of information. The shortness of the message forces you to be very brief, and this alone can create interest in those reading. Because tweets are so short, they often lead to frequent posting, which is excellent when you are looking to communicate with people and to get to know them. While Twitter is, by default, public, you can restrict the people who see your material with the ease of checking a box in your profile.

You will find that not only can you post tweets, you can also receive them. Once again, the immediate nature of this service lends greatly to its appeal. Want to follow someone's updates and see what they are up to with their business or life in general? Simply sign into your Twitter account, type in their Twitter address or username and click the "Follow" button. That's all there is to it.

The amount of time that spent reading the messages is very short, and you can be in contact with people a great deal more than you otherwise might be. In essence, you can get to know each other much more quickly than if you were just reading each other's blogs or profiles. The look and feel of an instant messaging service helps add to this ability. Think about it for a minute, do you feel more connected to those on your messenger list than the blogs you read? Twitter is the same way.

For many, whether they are looking for friends, clients, or someone to help them out with a problem or workload, getting in touch with others is important. With Twitter it has never been easier!

Click Here For More Great Tips!

About the Author

Click Here For More Social Networking Tips!

Getting to Know Twitter & Your Fellow Tweeps

By Amy Cacher

If you find yourself in a position that you need to understand your target customer as well as keep up with various ways of marketing to those potential customers, Twitter is one of the most powerful and popular tools out there right now! This new type of network communication has been taken up by companies and individuals alike in recent months and for good reason.

To get a better understanding of Twitter, lets first take a look at the format. Essentially, Twitter is a program that allows you to make very small, public posts. Because these posts are so limited (they max out at 140 characters) they can easily be sent to a number of different locations all at once. When you have written a Twitter, it can appear on the twitter website, on short message services, instant messaging sites or even on third-party applications like Facebook or Twitterific. Folks can even add a script to their blog or website to show their most recent posts and the posts of others! Your Twitter messages, also known tweets, will appear to anyone who has chosen to follow your updates.

There are several advantages to this type of communication. The first thing that you will discover is that it allows for a much more immediate relay of information. The shortness of the message forces you to be very brief, and this alone can create interest in those reading. Because tweets are so short, they often lead to frequent posting, which is excellent when you are looking to communicate with people and to get to know them. While Twitter is, by default, public, you can restrict the people who see your material with the ease of checking a box in your profile.

You will find that not only can you post tweets, you can also receive them. Once again, the immediate nature of this service lends greatly to its appeal. Want to follow someone's updates and see what they are up to with their business or life in general? Simply sign into your Twitter account, type in their Twitter address or username and click the Followbutton. That's all there is to it.

The amount of time that spent reading the messages is very short, and you can be in contact with people a great deal more than you otherwise might be. In essence, you can get to know each other much more quickly than if you were just reading each other's blogs or profiles. The look and feel of an instant messaging service helps add to this ability. Think about it for a minute, do you feel more connected to those on your messenger list than the blogs you read? Twitter is the same way.

For many, whether they are looking for friends, clients, or someone to help them out with a problem or workload, getting in touch with others is important. With Twitter it has never been easier!

About the Author

Do You need more help with Social Networking? Visit http://vickysvirtualoffice.com

Is Twitter a Powerful Marketing Tool?

By Amy Cacher

Whether you are just getting started with an online business or you have been around for a while & looking for a new way to network, have a look at what Twitter. Part chat program & part tiny blog, you will find that the Twitter interface is one that can alter the way you interact with your current customers & potential customers worldwide. Here are 5 reasons Twitter is a powerful marketing tool for online business owners like you.

1. It's Short, Sweet & To the Point

Have you ever heard the phrase, less is more? You'll find that one of the best things about Twitter is that it keeps all messages short & sweet. You'll have to give your customers & clients the gist of what's going on in short tweets (messages similar to instant messages) that allow their interest to be piqued in such a way as to make them investigate further. You won't bother them with long-winded messages that make them yawn & move on. Instead, you will be able to catch their attention quickly & make them require to know more.

2. Immediacy

Much like a blog or an RSS feed, you can get access to the people that use Twitter regularly. In some ways, this is like making sure that you can reach them no matter where they're, & you will find that this is important when you require to make marketing one of your biggest priorities. you are making sure that they have all of the latest updates to what you are doing & what's going on by basically sending a tweet their way.

3. Everyone's Doing It

In plenty of ways, Twitter is a social program over it is a marketing four, & you'll find that using Twitter can help you feel a great deal closer to your client base & others in your online community. If you are looking to make sure that they see you as a person than as basically a company or service, you'll find that Twitter encourages them to think of you as someone they can get to know. This can be important when it comes to establishing a customer base & customer loyalty.

4. You Get to Hear a Lot

Remember that it goes both ways; you can put information out on Twitter & you can also learn a lot . By following others Twitter accounts, if it looks like they have a lot to offer, you can keep in the know about various products, services, & other happenings online. This can be a great way to keep an eye on what's going on in order to keep yourself in the know of your industry.

5. Make Them Laugh

You can also use Twitter to tease people a little bit, in a fun way, of work! When you use Twitter, you have to keep your messages short, & in plenty of ways, a little mysterious. Pique their interest, joke around, & you'll find that you gain a lot more followers & hopefully website traffic & customers as a result.

Be warned, just as with any other social networking site, Twitter can quickly become addicting if you let it. Don't go overboard & get so involved in all the tweeting that it takes away from your intended intention. Used wisely Twitter can be a great & powerful marketing tool to help generate online business success.

About the Author

Looking for a New Clients, a Writer, Blog Installer,Va or Logo? Click here.

Flicker, Twitter, delicious; Web 2.0

By Sarbjot Singh

The Internet is alive with places to market your business, and more are coming on the scene each day. This can lead to hyperactive attempts to conduct comprehensive internet marketing 2.0 campaigns, but it is not always worth leaping onto each new bandwagon. Particularly if you have a limited budget.

However, some sites are leading the way in their field and do provide valuable opportunities for Online Public Relations (PR) and marketing at very little expense.

Social Bookmarks Delicious led the way back in 2003, offering every Internet user the chance to bookmark sites and content of interest at delicious and share those with other users. Delicious has grown from strength to strength and offers websites a valuable chance to gain backlinks and exposure. Others in a similar vein are Digg, Furl, Reddit, and Stumbleupon. You can easily access this audience by adding the appropriate code into the footer of your site, or after valuable content or articles, so that your visitor adds you to their list of social bookmarks.

Photo Galleries Flicker was one of the first sites that offered users the chance to share their photos with the rest of the world. It is worth creating a photo album of your company's products and photos, and where permissible allowing these photos to be used on other peoples websites, with an accreditation, particularly if the photo clearly shows your brand, logo, URL etc.

Twitter Once upon a time there was blogging, and now there is twitter. This is a seemingly meaningless application that allows users to send messages from their mobile phone or through a Web application on to the Twitter website (or your own) to say, What I am doing now. Twitter could prove to be one of those social networking experiences which dies out over time, or it could become part of your marketing toolbox.

For canny marketers however Twitter is being used as a tool which offers a very simple method to regularly inform customers about products, services etc, and to widen exposure of your company. Whether you twitter during the launch of a product, or twitter whilst at an exhibition, conference or awards ceremony, or use it as a mini-blog, or to announce a sale of your products, you can use this tool effectively to capture the interest of your customers and promote what you are doing with your business. A Senior Manager at Amazon uses it, and if he does, you can be sure that Amazon are finding value in it as a communication and marketing tool.

Whichever of the new social tools you decide to incorporate into your marketing strategy, you should ensure that they build on your current policies and fit your budget, and particularly the time available to you. A blog or twitter site that is full of enthusiasm one day and then abandoned the next does nothing for the image of your company.

About the Author

Did you find this article useful? For more useful tips & hints, Points to ponder and keep in mind, techniques & insights pertaining to Google Ad sense, Do please browse for more information at our website :-

http://www.seo-prediction.com
http://www.seo.reprintarticlesite.com

How Twitter Has Invaded Our Lives

By Alex Cleanthous

If you haven't been Twittering lately, then you haven't lived at all. It seems that Twitter - the website that promotes blogging on a tiny scale - has captured the attention of plenty of people with lots of diverse motives for using it.

At first glance you might wonder why everyone is so keen to use it. After all this really is blogging in a hurry - you get a mere 140 characters to say your piece, and that includes a link to another website if you want it.

But therein lies the attraction. It seems that a lot of people become intimidated or overwhelmed by the prospect of keeping up with the demands of a normal blog, whereas Twitter takes all those away by limiting the amount you can say. Of course there will always be those who join up and get started, only to abandon it as a waste of time just a few days later.

So are there rewards on the site for those who seek them, or is it just another social networking site?

Whatever you think of Twitter, it certainly looks like it's here to stay. It's also very forward thinking, giving you the chance to receive Tweets (the Twitterworld's name for one of its short blog posts) on your mobile phone. Quite why you would want to receive these when you could be following hundreds if not thousands of people is anyone's guess, but some people obviously find it a good addition to the overall service since it's still up and going.

As far as the website itself is concerned its quite basic in design, which really follows on from the simplicity of the idea behind it. It's not always the easiest of sites to navigate or find what you're looking for, but that doesn't seem to deter the merry band of Twitterers who are growing ever larger by the second.

And it looks like everyone is finding a different use for it - not least the number of internet marketers who use it to find an audience for their products and services, and let them know what's going on in their business lives.

What started as a socially based site has perhaps inevitably been spotted and used for other means by people wanting to sell things online. That's no bad thing, although some purists would probably argue that its abusing what Twitter was created for in the first place. So long as it's not done to excess, most people don't mind a bit of promotion - and that probably includes the Twitter staff themselves.

At the moment Twitter isn't on the same level as other sites such as MySpace and Facebook, but if it carries on growing as it has done, who's to say that it won't catch up? At the end of the day it has a unique function that simply isn't served anywhere else, and that is what is attracting huge amounts of people to sign up and start micro-blogging about whatever makes them happy.

About the Author

Web Profits specializes in search engine optimization, on-line marketing & web design, helping businesses generate profits from the Internet. For a free report on The Secrets of Online Marketing for Offline Businesses visit SEO.

How To Use Twitter For Marketing

By Darren Olander

Twitter is a relatively new web 2.0 site that is starting to gain a lot of popularity. That means that a lot of people have heard of it but it is also quite common to run into people who haven't heard of it.. yet. Twitter.com is this social site that encourages users to post often about what they are currently doing.

A lot of people are using it to improve their marketing reach, by being an active twitterer they gain followers who are interested in what they got going on. This means people being exposed to their updates on a regular basis. For example, if you have hundreds of followers in Twitter and you decide to post an affiliate link, that means that hundreds of people have instantly been exposed to your offer. In this article I will discuss ways to maximize Twitter for your marketing, and also a big mistake to be aware of.

In order to have a fan base per say of followers in Twitter you must be able to keep their interest in you and what you are doing now. "What are you doing?" is the whole foundation of what Twitter is about in the first place. Make sure to post daily if not several times throughout the day updates about what you are doing. The magical thing behind this is that many of your contacts will be able to feel like they know you so much better, will trust you more, and feel much more comfortable about working with you. On the other hand, when you follow others you can learn about them and their possible needs.

The big mistake to watch out for is only posting affiliate links or offers on your Twitter page. This looks like Spam and many people will see you as just abusing Twitter for your own personal gain. Think of it this way, if you would not want to invite your friends or family to keep up with you via Twitter then you are going about it all wrong. As with anything you send out or provide, ninety percent should be content and ten percent (at most) advertising. So this concept is quite simple... constantly post throughout the day what you are doing.. it is usually very simple and only takes a few seconds to post! Secondly, if you write articles or provide content online, provide a link for those in your Twitter posts. You may post many things within one day, but the last thing you post for the day is usually the most important because it will be there the longest. This means that your last post for the day should very well contain a link that you want your followers to see before your start Twittering again the next day!

Another part of Twitter is contributing. As with any social site it should be a give and take relationship. Notice that give comes first... the more you give the more people will want to work with you and the more attention you will receive. Make sure to read and follow other users in Twitter. If you read something interesting or helpful then make sure to reply and say so, or even put a link for it on your Twitter so that you are directing others to more quality content. This can also be as simple as connecting with other users, if they know you are reading their Twitter page they will be much more likely to check out what you have going on too.

To get started in Twitter you should first invite contacts who aren't using Twitter and also find contacts who are already using Twitter so that you can start following them and also start getting people to follow you. Twitter has a nice invite and find feature that makes this incredibly easy. To grow your reach even more you can start following people who follow or are followed by the people who follow you.. or that you follow. You might need to read that sentence again.. but basically you can find other users to connect with that are already connected to other users.

Now for a big tip. If you really want to maximize the potential with Twitter, you should make sure to take advantage of any plug-ins or sites that support Twitter. Here are three, but I'm sure there will be many more in the future if not already. Squidoo allows you to input your Twitter account info into your Squidoo account and then it can automatically post updates to your Twitter account when you create or update Squidoo lenses. Facebook has an application called Twitter, it automatically updates your Facebook status when you make a Twitter post. The other tool is a free WordPress plug-in called TweetMyBlog that allows you to create a two-way connection from your blogs to Twitter. TweetMyBlog allows you to use a widget on your Wordpress blogs that will display your current Twitter feed.. that way all visitors to your blog can look at the widget and see a running feed of your latest Twitter posts. If they click on that they will be brought to your Twitter page. In addition, when you make a new post to your blog, TweetMyBlog will automatically make a post to your Twitter page with a link to your latest blog post. Imagine the extra exposure you can receive by using these tools that help people see more of what you are doing.

Lastly, have fun! Twitter is a social site... so interact and enjoy!

About the Author

Darren Olander is dedicated to teaching others how to create a success online through internet network marketing strategies. He is a site owner, article writer, coach & marketing consultant enjoying the benefits of working full time from home. Learn more about him at http://www.darrenolander.com

Micro-Blogging on Twitter

By Penny Sansevieri

There's a hot new trend going on right now and it's called micro-blogging. So what's a micro-blog? And moreover, what's Twitter? Twitter is a micro-blogger platform that allows users to create entries that are only 140 characters in length. These entries are referred to as "tweets."

Originally designed to keep friends and family up to date on what you're doing, Twitter can also be a great place to share your latest book project, promotional ideas as well as interacting with fellow tweets (folks who twitter) and writers. And yes, you can have a blog and a Twitter page. I have both but I feed my blog into my Twitter site so that my Twitter page gets updated each time I add new content to my blog. There's an easy application to add your blog feed to Twitter, it takes just minutes to do. Head on over to: Twitterfeed.

To sign up for a Twitter account just complete their short sign up form. Remember to brand yourself! This is important. Once you create a Twitter account you can't go back and change your name so find something that works for you. Maybe it's fictionwriter or businesswriter or whatever you want. My Twitter page is bookgal which is fun play on words for what I do (and what I love). Once you have a Twitter account you can immediately start tweeting. The service is completely free and you can also keep up with other people's tweets by "following" them. Their micro-blog entries will show up on your Twitter home page so you can easily keep track of them. You can also be notified by phone when they add a tweet. You can twitter from anywhere, even your phone. I've been known to twitter from my blackberry.

Why on Earth Would you Want to Twitter?

When Twitter first started, people were a little perplexed. I mean why on earth would you want to blog in 140 characters? Well since the site emerged in 2006, it's grown enormously in popularity. With Twitter pages from sites like CNN and every one of the political candidates, the site's popularity can't be overstated. Nor can its applications for the future. Also, even if you don't have a ton of people following your tweets, keep in mind that Twitter search sites are popping up everywhere. This means that if you tweet using keywords that matter to your reader/market, you could be found and followed! For one such search site check out: summarize. Also, if you're trying to gauge the popularity of a certain word or phrase and how often it's being used or referred to, you can head on over to Tweet Volume and find out. Just plug in your search term or terms and up will pop a list of results!

Most Well-Known Twitter Users

* Many organizations (such as the Los Angeles Fire Department) have embraced the technology and put it to use in situations such as the October 2007 California wildfires.

* Higher education is also using the technology to relay important information to students in a more timely manner. The University of Texas at San Antonio College of Engineering is one such example.

* Several U.S. presidential campaigns use Twitter as a publicity mechanism, Ron Paul, John Edwards, Barack Obama, and Hillary Clinton all have Twitter pages.

* Media outlets such as CNN have also started using Twitter to break news.

How to Use Twitter Effectively

If you've pondered using Twitter but aren't sure how to use it effectively, here are some quick tips to give you some great twittering-ideas:

* Teach stuff - teach a little mini-lesson on Twitter. Delve into your area of expertise or just talk about book publishing and how to get published.

* Showcase your book - don't do this in a "my book is so fabulous" kind of way but offer to give advice (like I mention in Teach Stuff) or share with your Twitter followers how the promotion of the book is going.

* Use Twitter as a news source: you can easily announce news both from your world (as long as it relates to your topic) and from the world of your expertise. So for example I've done tweets on book industry stuff, breaking news, etc.

* Widen your network - follow other Twitter folk, this will not only give you some ideas for your own "tweets" but it's a great way to network with other writers or professionals.

* Keep the buzz going when you're on the move - it's hard to keep blogging when you're on the road (trust me, I know this first hand) - so when I travel, I tweet. I share what I'm doing, what's happening in my world and try to offer insight and advice.

* Market yourself - remember that while Twitter may seem like a fun little tool, it's also a great way to market yourself. Just like the ideas we mention above, there are a hundred+ more things you can do.

Golden Rules of Twitter:

Here are a few rules to live by when tweeting:

* Be Original, useful and helpful.

* Every Tweet counts (don't tell people you're washing your cat) don't just tweet on useless stuff or you'll lose followers.

* Ask questions: you've got a network (or you want one) now use it! Ask questions, take surveys, get your followers involved in your message and marketing!

* It's not all about you (again, back to the cat) people want to know useful stuff, I know, it's getting repetitive but there's a reason: it's important.

* Promote your Twitter account in your email signature line and on your blog.

* Network: don't expect your followers to grow if you're not following other people. Network, search for others in your area and follow them.

* Personal is ok. Even though I said not to post useless information it's still not a bad idea to (from time to time) post a personal Tweet or two. Provide value and twitter-followers will beat a path to your door.

* Keep Twittering, followers will come if you keep updating your Twitter account.

About the Author

Penny C. Sansevieri, CEO and founder of Author Marketing Experts, Inc., is a book marketing and media relations expert whose company has developed some of the most cutting-edge book marketing campaigns. Visit AME.

Twitter Marketing!

By Albert, Blueprint mentor

If you haven't yet created a Twitter account you're really missing out.

This service has exploded in growth in the past few months and I don't see it slowing down anytime soon. There are now MILLIONS of users and it's becoming mainstream. I've been running some interesting tests and I'm already seeing some great traffic results -- far greater than the traffic from Facebook or any other "Web 2.0" service.

Facebook and the others certainly have their place, but Twitter is more powerful. At first I didn't really "get it" but now I do and my traffic stats don't lie. IT WORKS. As a communications tool, Twitter is probably only 2nd to Email right now. It's a great way to network with people as well as to drive visitors to any of your sites, blog posts, etc.

BUT DON'T WAIT...

Create a Twitter account NOW and start 'following' people you want. Others will eventually follow you in return. Observe how others post and you'll quickly learn the culture, etiquette, and uses for Twitter.

It's not rocket science. In fact, it's a lot of fun.

You really need to start today because the sooner you start the sooner your followers list will start growing and more people will see your posts -- which will then virally grow from there.

VERY IMPORTANT

MAKE SURE TO FOLLOW ME! (I'm actively posting all the time.)

Create an account then go here: http://twitter.com/blueprintmentor

Click the "Follow" link that shows under my photo. That's it. Everytime I post you'll see it in your main "timeline" area.

* After you click to "Follow" me look at the right-hand side of my profile page. Click the blue "Followers" link and you can see all the people currently following my posts. Follow some of these other marketers so you can get involved.

Twitter is extremely VIRAL. When you make posts (called "tweets") they can be exposed to all the friends followers) of others. Then they can choose to follow you.

I think Twitter is going to really evolve into a "must use" marketing tool. It's a great way to announce you've just made a new blog post, released a new product, or anything else you're up to.

I'm already seeing 400+ visitors each time I make a tweet that I've made a new blog post.

So trust me, this is no flash in the pan. In fact, this may be one of the most powerful marketing tools ever -- it just depends how it evolves. But so far you'd be crazy not to use it. It's producing great results.

Take 2 minutes to create an account -- check you'll want to do it now so you can at least get your name before someone else takes it. Or your company or product name, etc.

Just go to http://www.Twitter.com

Then visit my page at: http://twitter.com/blueprintmentor And click "Follow" that is displayed under my photo. (That's all there is to it.)

See you on Twitter!

* You'll definitely want to be following me on Twitter because I'm going to be doing some really cool stuff with it soon.

Yours For Online Profits,

Albert, $200Blueprint mentor

About the Author

Hello world. I am a mentor for 200blueprint and work successful in the marketing online.

Using 'Twitter' to help your Affiliate Marketing

By Ryan Allaire

Twitter and Affiliate Marketing??

Hey,

This is just an update of an affiliate tool I've been using and I'm noticing it's a HUGE Profit maker- and NO cost!! It's a site that allows you to send only 140 characters- so the message isn't some long drawn out email and, you can just get to the point on this virtual message board. This allows you to give personal friends and clients updates from time to time on things you're doing throughout the day.. or the best part that I like- is getting CRAZY information on building and growing your online marketing biz- which relates to you guessed it- Affiliate Marketing which = Sales!!

http://theaffiliateblog.com/twitter-and-affiliate-marketing

It's called Twitter.. http://www.Twitter.com

So, I found a social networking site that is very easy to use. You just click follow and start following people, and then people start following you in return (human nature- seeing what other people are up to;).. it's pretty sweet- not only your updating your closest friends through Twitter, but you can also share tips and tricks on what's working for you in the online marketplace. I'm seeing people use this to generate an extra 5 figures a week, and building their client base in all nitches(YouTube Celebs= are increasing viewers, information marketing =building email lists and clients, Realtors = staying in touch with clients, so on and so on.)

http://theaffiliateblog.com/twitter-and-affiliate-marketing

All you need to do is go to http://www.Twitter.com create an account and just start connecting with people.. It's fun, easy, fast, and even profitable!!

Check mine out: http://www.Twitter.com/RyanAllaire

Once you sign up add me as a friend! You simply put an sign in front of the persons screen name to search In my case-mine is RyanAllaire . I follow all the gurusto be up on the latest trends online, and have that marketing advantage!! Well I fully recommend it and let me know if you're having any TwitterSuc-cess!! Can't wait to see you on Twitter!!! Let me know that your following me so I can do the same in return!! As Always, To Your Success!!

The   Affiliate   Blog   Ryan   Allaire
Http://www.TheAffiliateBlog.com

PS: If we have enough interest I can set up interviews with people using Twitter and making the income we all want and DESERVE!!

About the Author

Ryan Allaire is the brains behind http://TheAffiliateBlog.com He has partnered on several multi-million dollar deals and has a huge interest in helping others find FREE Traffic to their websites- to make the Affiliate sales they deserve!! For more info please visit:
http://theaffiliateblog.com/twitter-and-affiliate-marketing

Getting The Most Out of Your Followers on Twitter

By Matthew Bredel

Twitter doesn't sound like much. It suggests that you tell the world what you're doing in 140 characters or less. So what? How are people using this social marketing tool to make more money online?

What You Need To Know: Follow and Be Followed!

The key to twitter is to follow and be followed. If you're on the site talking about what you're doing to nobody and not finding what anyone else is doing, it's sort of useless and rather boring. Once you get a few followers and start following a person, that's when the buzz starts. You can update your status on the web, via instant messaging client or via a third party tool like Twhirl that lets you use twitter from your own desktop. You can follow and be followed on your cell phone as well and be plugged in to the Twitterverse on the go.

You have a profile page that lets you manage the tool and lets people look you up to see what you're all about in a few lines and with a URL. It's the "What are you doing" section that counts.

Your Twitter friends or peeps (a.k.a your Tweeps) all carry on conversations with or without you and when you pop in and chime into various conversations, it gets rather lively. People ask questions, answer questions and share URLS of what they're doing, what they find interesting and what they want opinions on.

There's also the public timeline that tells you what other people are doing and you can search on that for more followers or conversations to eavesdrop on. It's like a virtual water cooler that you can stop into during the day and check in with your tweeps.

Use Twitter when you:

- Post an update to your blog - Want answers to a technical question - Want to vent - Want to tell people what you're having for lunch (seriously, that can sparks some very interesting questions) and more.

You can also send direct private messages as well as respond to people both directly but also publicly. The more interesting of a Tweet you post, the more likely people will follow you and re-tweet. A re-tweet is when you post a URL and someone likes it so they share it by tweeting or re-tweeting it to their followers. Do you see how it can become a benefit to you in an area like affiliate marketing, product launches and technical challenges you need help with?

You can also post Twitter feeds on your website so that people can follow you, read your conversations, see who you're following and visit their posts or URLS so it becomes a very viral way to share and communicate and even to collaborate.

The downside to Twitter

Not only is the tool currently growing at such a fast rate that it goes down regularly but there is another downside and that's productivity. Sadly there's almost always a downside to social networking and bookmarking tools and as with many others, Twitter can be a time waster if you're not careful so it's important to use it and have fun but also to set limits for yourself.

About the Author

To learn more about how social marketing tools can help you and your online money making efforts, visit TheWebReviewer; a resource for making money online, affiliate marketing and more.

Web 2.0 - Flickr, Twitter, delicious etc

By Phil Robinson

The Internet is alive with places to market your business, and more are coming on the scene each day. This can lead to hyperactive attempts to conduct comprehensive internet marketing 2.0 campaigns, but it is not always worth leaping onto each new bandwagon. Particularly if you have a limited budget.

However, some sites are leading the way in their field and do provide valuable opportunities for Online Public Relations (PR) and marketing at very little expense.

Social Bookmarks Del.icio.us led the way back in 2003, offering every Internet user the chance to bookmark sites and content of interest at del.icio.us and share those with other users. Delicious has grown from strength to strength and offers websites a valuable chance to gain backlinks and exposure. Others in a similar vein are Digg, Furl, Reddit, and Stumbleupon. You can easily access this audience by adding the appropriate code into the footer of your site, or after valuable content or articles, so that your visitor adds you to their list of social bookmarks.

Photo Galleries Flickr was one of the first sites that offered users the chance to share their photos with the rest of the world. It is worth creating a photo album of your company's products and photos, and where permissible allowing these photos to be used on other people's websites, with an accreditation, particularly if the photo clearly shows your brand, logo, URL etc.

Twitter Once upon a time there was blogging, and now there is twitter. This is a seemingly meaningless application that allows users to send messages from their mobile phone or through a Web application on to the Twitter website (or your own) to say, "What I am doing now". Twitter could prove to be one of those social networking experiences which dies out over time, or it could become part of your marketing toolbox.

For canny marketers however Twitter is being used as a tool which offers a very simple method to regularly inform customers about products, services etc, and to widen exposure of your company. Whether you twitter during the launch of a product, or twitter whilst at an exhibition, conference or awards ceremony, or use it as a mini-blog, or to announce a sale of your products, you can use this tool effectively to capture the interest of your customers and promote what you are doing with your business. A Senior Manager at Amazon uses it, and if he does....you can be sure that Amazon are finding value in it as a communication and marketing tool.

Whichever of the new social tools you decide to incorporate into your marketing strategy, you should ensure that they build on your current policies and fit your budget, and particularly the time available to you. A blog or twitter site that is full of enthusiasm one day and then abandoned the next does nothing for the image of your company.

About the Author

Phil Robinson is an experienced online marketing consultant and Founder of ClickThrough Marketing - an international Search Engine Marketing & Internet Marketing agency. Specialists in Search Engine Optimization, Pay Per Click Marketing, Online PR, Social Marketing & Website Conversion Strategies.

Twitter - Are You A Twitter Addict?

By John v

Many people have now discovered the power of twitter both for entertainment purposes, as well as to make some money online. Yes you can actually earn a crust using this little tool.

Although twitter is fairly new it is gaining popularity fairly quickly. If you are not away twitter is also amazing for marketing purposes because Twitter does require you to update your profile quite frequently so there is a little "work" involved. It's fun but Google loves the new content that you add.

Some of the big time marketers are raving about the new web 2.0 environment, however this is fast becoming one of their favorites. That's why you will see alot of these big names on twitter sharing their lives and individual experiences.

Twitter will give you lots of tools and opportunity to it's pretty easy to integrate twitter with your regular moneymaking programs. That's what makes it so much fun. The opportunities are almost limitless.

The best tip about becoming successful with twitter is to mimic those same twitter pages that have big followings and are successful.

I've been using Twitter for quite a while now (1,552 updates). I've been using it for a while to stay on top of trends, drive traffic, stay in touch with friends, help customers, and much more.

You can make alot of money on twitter if you do things right.

To make the experience complete you need to try a few excellent Twitter "accessories" as well

Give these a try and see if it increase your experience or help increase you marketing.

Twhirl - Desktop Twitter client built in Adobe Air. http://www.Twhirl.org

TwitterFeed - RSS to Twitter http://www.TwitterFeed.com

Quotably - Follows Twitter conversations for better context http://www.Quotably.com

Tweetburner - Track what happens to the links you share on Twitter http://www.TweetBurner.com

About the Author

John Has Helped Many People Achieve Success Online By Giving Them The Lastest And Greatest Marketing Info Visit :- http://www.moneytreeprofits.com

Everyone Is All A-Twitter About Twitter

By Jennifer Horowitz

I personally have been Tweeting for a few months. But I use the phrase "tweeting for a few months" loosely. I haven't been all that consistent with it, and I definitely didn't have a strategy. I just thought it was kind of cool.

Recently I've started paying more attention to it for a few reasons; my mother-in-law was at a librarian conference recently and attended a session on Twitter. I got into a conversation with her about it, and then the next day I saw John Reese's email about Twitter. It seems like there is a lot of twittering about Twitter going on. What is Twitter?

According to the Twitter FAQ, "Twitter is for staying in touch and keeping up with friends no matter where you are or what you're doing."

Wikipedia says, "Twitter is a free social networking and mi-cro-blogging service that allows users to send updates via SMS, instant messaging, email, to the Twitter website, or any one of the multitude of Twitter applications now available".

Basically Twitter asks the question, "What are you doing?" and allows you to send a short update (your tweets are limited to 140 characters) to your followers (family, friends, colleagues, customers, potential customers etc).

Twitter allows you to send and receive updates (also called tweets) via your browser, email, instant messaging clients and SMS (using your cell phone). No matter where you are, you can tweet!

I haven't been following Twitter since day 1, so I'm not going to comment on its evolution but I will speculate that as its popularity grows, as more and more marketers use it, 2 things are inevitable:

1. Rules on Twitter etiquette will continue to evolve as we learn what we like and dislike about it, and as we respond to the inevitable abuse of Twitter (don't mean to sound negative but it happens with each exciting new opportunity ' people end up abusing it).

2. More and more companies will jump on board and try to get in on the conversation.

Start Twittering, (or is it Tweeting?)

Remember, when you first join Twitter, it can feel like a lonely place. When you aren't following anyone and no one is following you, you may find yourself asking "what is the point?" I've heard so many people say they just don't get it. In fact, I've said that myself.

The key is to find the Tweets you want to follow so you can keep your finger on the pulse of your niche. The next key is to start building your followers. More on that in a minute.

How can Twitter help your business?

The more contact you have with a potential customer, the more likely you are to get their business. You can stay "top of mind" through Twitter. Let them know what's new in your industry, in your company etc. You become a source of quick news flashes for them.

Here are just a few of the benefits of Twitter: - It reminds people that you exist

- It shows people you have something to say

- It shows them that you are human

- It allows you to mention new offers, sales and breaking news immediately

- It allows you to form a more casual relationship

- You can use Twitter to promote your social bookmarking submissions.

- You can ask for referrals, suggestions, feedback and help, and people will respond.

Twitter is also fun and is contributing to the new language we are constantly developing. For example "Twitterference" ' the intrusion of twitter updates on your phone making it hard to have a conversation on your phone.

Finding Followers:

Start by reaching out to your friends, family, mailing list etc. You can also add your Twitter link to your email signature line; add links to your website and Blog. Mention your Twitter account in your newsletter.

Twitter Rules

One cardinal rule (that is in your best interest to follow): if you use Twitter as a pure sales tool, you will lose followers quickly. As with all forms of social media, it is about creating a conversation and sharing news ' it's not all about you shoving your sales message down their throats.

Tweets are limited to 140 characters. This is to allow them to be easily sent over mobile SMS systems.

You aren't able to embed HTML with the exception of hyperlinks. (But they are no-follow links, so they won't help you in your SEO quest for backlinks) Bonus: Twitter automatically uses the TinyURL service to shorten links.

Don't tweet too much, or too little. There is no magic number and it varies according to your audience. Some people say don't update more than once per hour. Others say not more than once or twice a day. I tend to be in the once or twice a day camp. If there is breaking news and some days you just have to update more often then it's OK. If your tweets are valuable information people will be more tolerant of frequent updates.

On the other hand if you are too quiet, people have nothing to follow so make sure you find that balance and tweet just enough to keep people informed but not annoyed.

Don't forget that your profile shows a history of all your tweets, so if a new person comes along and sees that you don't have many tweets they may decide you aren't worthy of following. Also if your past tweets aren't informative or interesting, you lose some potential followers.

You'll find that sometimes you get involved in personal conversation with someone. Try to avoid doing too much of this. Not everyone will be interested in your personal communications. If you do need to do this, put the @ symbol in front of somebody's name ' this indicates that this message is for them.

One thing to keep in mind about personal conversation tweets - some people who are following you may not be following the person you are talking to. This means they get only one half of the conversation. One suggestion is to word your tweet so that spectators have an idea of what you are talking about. That way, they can feel more included in the conversation.

Trust and Twitter

With so much hype in marketing, people are really looking for a company that can trust. You can build trust with prospects by allowing them to get to know you, and by providing them with information. Twitter allows you to do just that.

A great tip: look at your own Tweet history ' is the information valuable, does it build trust? Would you want to follow yourself?

Get tweeting!

It may take some trial and error, and you probably want to check out what others are tweeting about to get a feel for the style. But don't spend too long lurking ' check it out and then jump on in.

About the Author

Jennifer Horowitz is the Director of Marketing and co-owner of http://www.EcomBuffet.com Since 1998, her expertise in online marketing and Search Engine Optimization (SEO) has helped clients increase revenue and achieve their business goals. Jennifer has written a downloadable book on Search Engine Optimization and has been published in many SEO and marketing publications. Jennifer can be reached at Jennifer@ecombuffet.com

Building A Twitter Following

By Jeff Tippett

Lots of people ask for tips on building a follower base in Twitter. If you are wondering about this, you should also ask yourself another question: what's your goal? My colleague and I are both avid Twitterers. However, we Tweet for entirely different purposes, and our communities of followers is radically different because we have different objectives.

Why I Tweet: JeffTippett I Tweet in an attempt to build community. Admittedly I'm that annoying guy in the line at Starbucks that's asking how your day is goingï¿½"what exciting events are coming up in your life, etc. I have an innate desire to chat and build horizontal relationships. If you don't believe meï¿½"just ask my colleagues! This natural tendency plays out for me in Twitter. I'm seeking a large group so I can learn from them, help them when they need help, and ask for help as I need it. Thus, a large horizontal group of followers is important to me. Of course, I'm always excited when a few of the relationships become vertical relationships.

Why I Tweet: Glowbird For me, Twitter is all about breaking news, field-related links, and strategic partners. So I follow major bloggers and other news sources like Techmeme, Mashable, Jowyang, New York Times, and even an NBC cameraman who twitters his impressions before the news stories hit. My favorite corporate Twitterers are those who not only use Twitter to RSS me links to news, but who also speak as individuals. In addition, I want a strong local community of peers, so I will add people whose profiles let me know they are geographically nearby, particularly if we share industry or personal affinities.

My Strategy: JeffTippett Ultimately, I find followers by following people of interest to me. I'm into social media, cycling, working out, running, politics, and social networking (well, plus a few others). I look for people that are talking about these issues. My hope is that they will follow me as well. I've started noticing a trend that helps me predict whether or not the person will return the follow. If they have a higher amount of people that they are following compared to the number that's following them I find the odds play in my favor that they will follow me. Conversely, if they have a lower amount of people they are following versus following them, the chances are slim to acquire a new follower. I've even asked my followers (those with whom I have a close relationship) to Tweet out to their networks to follow @jefftippett. A great time to do this is after you've done something to help them. It doesn't hurt to ask!

My Strategy: Glowbird For breaking news and field-related links, my strategy is often to work backwards: I look on internet sites that I like (for example, Mashable.com or MarketingPilgrim.com) to see if I can find people there who Twitter (like Pete Cashmore or Andy Beal). I also use Twitter-specific search engines like Terraminds.com to find businesses or people on Twitter. For local links, I look on wikis, get connected at events, and find people to connect with by browsing the profiles of followers of my other friends on Twitter.

A List of Where to Look and How to Add â€¢ Twitter's public timeline. Peruse the feed for conversations that interest you. Then check out a specific Twitterer's posts to see if they are a match for your goals. â€¢ Other people's followers. Check out your friends' followers. You may share common interests or goals. You can even ask your friends to invite their networks to follow you. â€¢ Traditional networking events. Ask people if they use Twitter and exchange Twitter names so that you can add each other. â€¢ Other social networks. Put a link to your Twitter account in other social sites like StumbleUpon, Digg, LinkedIn, LastFM, or Facebook. Often people that you like or are connected with there will also opt to follow you in Twitter. â€¢ Blogs and other sites you love. Where do you love to go on the internet? Is someone on the site offering a Twitter link or feed? Look in bio sections to find links for your favorite bloggers and add them. â€¢ Twitter search engines, aggregators, and specialty sites. Use Terraminds.com to search for subjects and people on Twitter. Watch for great twitters on StrawPollNow.com or Tweet140.com. Look at Twitterverse.com and click through to keyword conversations that engage your interest. Then add the people who are saying things you would like to hear. â€¢ Your email. Add a signature to your emails that includes a link to your Twitter account. Often people will clickï¿½"if for no other reasonï¿½"out of curiosity. Those that already Twitter may follow you. â€¢ Engage in the timeline conversation. Jump into the conversation of your current followers. The best tweets are helpful, friendly, and funny. If your friends enjoy and respond to your comments, then their followers will have the opportunity to see your tweets. If the conversation interests them, many times they will view your account and opt to follow. Tweet new followers and ask them a question. Chances are they will answer and then their followers have the opportunity to see your name and potentially follow you.

Set a goal and make it happen. Your goal may be higher or lower based on your objective. There are plenty of ways to make it happen!

About the Author

Jeff Tippett is the Outreach Strategist for Calvert Holdings, Inc. based in Cary, NC. He attended graduate and undergraduate school at East Carolina University, Greenville, NC. He may be reached at jeff.tippett@calvertholdings.com. He blogs at www.calvertcreative.com and is active on Twitter at www.twitter.com/jefftippett.

How To Use Twitter To Generate Traffic

By Nelson Tan

Twitter is still a relatively new social networking site, and there are still thousands of marketers who are not using it to its full potential. Some are not using it at all. As with just about any other social networking site you can mention, you have to put in the work at the start to establish yourself as a credible, helpful contributor who is there to do more than just give a sales message and win customers. Using Twitter is an art form all of its own, and is totally unlike anything you will do anywhere else.

The short length of the messages you are allowed to send means that you have to approach the task in a completely different way. The underlying principle does not change, however, and if you are looking to build a long term business presence, you will need to take a long-term view and work to build up your network of friends. These friends can see your twits on their Twitter home page, so it is well worth making the effort to cultivate as many as you can. You are allowed to put links in your twits, so you will need to restrain yourself from getting carried away and posting links too often.

As ever, it takes a bit of work and a bit of thought to use Twitter effectively. Make sure that your twits are of value and interesting. If you can keep abreast of breaking news, and the latest trends in your area of expertise, you can build up a reputation as being someone to watch out for. This will keep you on peoples friend lists, and give you the chance to broadcast an occasional message about your own website or profile which will encourage them to visit. Driving social network traffic is never quick or easy, but you can build up a reputation which will result in regular visitors to your site, who have every chance of becoming regular customers.

About the Author

Nelson Tan is the webmaster behind Internet Mastery Center. Download $347 worth of FREE Internet Marketing gifts at http://www.internetmasterycenter.com

Twitter for Business Communication

By Jeff Tippett

My Confession... Hi, my name is Jeff, and I'm a Twitter-holic!

So exactly what is Twitter? Twitter is a free online social networking service used to send/receive short messages within a specified group. Very much like sending an email to a distribution list, a Twitter post conveys a message to a predetermined list. However, the message must be a short, concise thought; 140 characters or less, to be precise. Twitter's homepage self defines Twitter as: "... a service for friends, family, and co-workers to communicate and stay connected through the exchange of quick, frequent answers to one simple question: What are you doing?" Twitter offers the option of viewing content on your Twitter homepage or receiving notifications on your mobile device.

Why I tried Twitter... Although friends had told me about Twitter, I ended up venturing to the site only after reading a blog about it. My argument against Twitter was blogging was sufficient...why would anyone need to microblog? However, my curiosity had been piqued, and I had to know why people were raving about it.

Why I liked Twitter... I found that Twitter is extremely contagious. Before long I was checking out Obama's Twitter account, reading Social Media Club's postings, and following CNN's account with notifications to my phone so I could stay up on the latest breaking news. It had me hooked! I wanted to know what people were doing. I was craving the communication.

But Twitter for Business? How Twitter can Move Your Business... How could my business benefit by sharing (sending/receiving) concise information with a group of people? Currently, most Twitterers seem to use it for personal socializing, for communicating their life with their friends. However, Twitter does provide new tools that can help move your business. Here are five examples:

* Transmit Instantaneous Messages and Log Information: The other day I spoke with someone that is part of a team that goes into businesses to work on networks. While working they send out Twitters to each other announcing what they are doing. Everyone who is a part of the team can see the same information and respond if needed. In addition, the messages are logged on the Twitter site. All communication is retrievable for future references.

* Drive Traffic to a Blog and/or Website: When this article goes live, I'll let my friends and associates know -- and hear their feedback -- by Twitter. I also drive traffic to other articles, sites, and information that might be useful to people in my Twitter network, knowing they will do the same for me.

* Discover New and Developing Ideas: By using Twitter to follow thought leaders in your industry you can stay in touch with new and emerging ideas. Short ideas and thoughts will be broadcast in an attempt to solicit feedback. Many bloggers will list their Twitter accounts on their blogs -- by following the person in Twitter you can gather new information even before it hits the blog. Look at this Twitter from rickklau announcing a new wiki and asking for help developing it: Need help with a high-visibility political site - not candidate-centric - in the next couple days. E-mail me rick@rklau.com if interested.

* Fuel New Ideas: Often as I read the Twitters of thought leaders I will begin to develop new ideas. In other words, the Twitters can be springboards for your own creative thinking. Here's a Tweet from gaping void in reflection of the Microsoft/Yahoo takeover: Still not convinced that a MSFT+Yahoo merger is enough to get in Google's way, long-term.

* Discover Breaking News: Since I communicate for a living I find it helpful to learn of breaking news. These news events often provide a catalyst for initiating conversation with people that I'm meeting. Here's a sample from newsmediajim while at the White House: budget chairman Spratt has just received the President's budget. at cursory glance, he didn't seem impressed

The Formula: No matter how you use Twitter in your business the basic formula remains the same: 1. Build/join a network 2. Read/send relevant messages

Not a definitive solution set, this list provides a catalyst for discovering ways that Twitter can move business. Businesses need effective communication, and Twitter can offer ways to communicate small messages to an emerging distribution list.

So, What are you doing?

About the Author

Jeff Tippett is the Outreach Strategist for Calvert Holdings, Inc., a privately held company with corporate offices in Cary, NC. He is an author, professional speaker, and entrepreneur. He attended graduate and undergraduate school at East Carolina University, Greenville, NC. He blogs at calvertcreative.blogspot.com and Twitters at twitter.com/jefftippett. He may be reached directly at jeff.tippett@calvertholdings.com or 919.854.4453.

Various Ways To Use Twitter On Your iPhone

By Graham Williams

Perhaps one of the main reasons so many people buy the iPhone is for the fact that it allows you to stay connected to the world in so many dynamic ways. Instead of simply using the phone to connect with your friends, you can do so through text messaging and even e-mail. However, one of the best ways to keep your online life moving, even when you're on the move, is by using social networking sites.

Many of the popular social networking sites allow you to access their site through your cell phone, however, the quality of service that you will get through your cell phone isn't always desirable. One of the best social networking sites that you can control when you are on the move is Twitter.

Twitter is based off of a basic concept to keep friends and family connected, without having to use extensive steps to communicate with them. When you own an iPhone, there are several tips that you can follow to keep your use of Twitter as seamless as possible. Perhaps one of the easiest ways to stay connected with Twitter through your iPhone is through your SMS system, or through text messaging. This is a very convenient way to keep updates about what you're doing to all of your friends and family, and all it takes is typing a short message through your SMS screen and sending it to a specific number. It is very easy to set this up on your iPhone, all you have to do is make sure you verify your phone number on Twitter's website, and then you can start sending updates to the people who matter, no matter where you are.

Another great way to keep your Twitter site updated is through visiting their mobile website. When you have an iPhone, you are probably going to be on the Internet more than you could possibly imagine. Whether you are in a waiting room, sitting in class or on a bus, you will be checking your e-mail and other popular sites. Of course, if you have a Twitter account, than you will want to update your status while killing time.

You can do this in a special website that was specifically designed to be used on your cell phone. You will be able to update your account, view your friends account and do everything else that you normally would, but now, it's on your cell phone.

In today's world it seems that we are busier than ever before, thus making the need to stay connected to those you care about extremely important. One way to keep in touch with your friends and family is through having a great cell phone, such as the iPhone. However, also being a part of an online social networking community, like Twitter, you will be able to keep your friends and family in-the-know, without having to worry about spending unnecessary amounts of time on the phone.

The greatest aspect of the iPhone is the fact that it streamlines all forms of communication, whether it be through text messaging or with checking your e-mail, the iPhone will take any hassle out of communicating with the world around you.

About the Author

For all the latest information and downloads for IPhone Click Here This amazing site will change the way you use your iPhone forever!!

Twitter For Musicians and Bands: A How-To Guide

Part of the beauty of Twitter is that it can be many things to many people. As part of my effort to recruit as many people to Twitter as possible, I decided that I should write posts about how Twitter can be used in different situations. For example, of course you can just use Twitter to make plans with your friends, but the interactivity of Twitter can be very useful for people in all sorts of different professions. I'm going to attempt to come up with as many different uses for it as I can and I'm going to start with the one I feel (for better or worse) qualified the most to talk about: using Twitter to promote your band or music.

Your Fans Really Do Care What You're Doing
Believe it or not, if you've been making music for a while, you've probably accumulated a not-insignificant group of fans who are interested in what you do on a daily basis. These are the fans that download all your songs (whether you want them to or not), go to all your shows and buy all your t-shirts. Every band has these, no matter how long you've been around or how bad your music is. These are the people that you can cater to with Twitter.

I suggest updating at least twice a day. Once when you get up you should post what you're going to be doing that day, whether or not it's related to your music, and once when your day is done to let them know how it went. Believe me, if Cedric and Omar from The Mars Volta or Daft Punk were on Twitter, you better believe I would be following them and would get super excited whenever they updated, even if it was just to let me know that they were eating a bowl of Cheerios.

Promoting Your Shows

Twitter can be an extremely effective promotional tool because you can ask people to come to your shows on several different occasions. If you are booking a tour, I suggest updating on Twitter when the dates are finalized and linking to the posted dates on your web site. Also, the day before the show, as well as the day of, you can update reminding everyone to come out to see you.

If you have enough fans and followers, you could make them feel extra special by having exclusive shows or after parties that you only mention on Twitter. Once your fans find out that you are having these secret events, they will start following you on Twitter, thereby increasing your reach.

Take Requests

Since Twitter makes it so easy to interact with your fans, why not ask them what they want to hear when they come to your show? Maybe you've been neglecting to play an old fan favorite. Twitter is an easy way to find out what your fans want to hear, straight from the source. All they have to do is either direct message you or reply to you using the @ symbol.

Twitter-Exclusive Downloads

Say thank you to your biggest fans by giving your Twitter followers the heads up on exclusive new songs and videos. Posting a link on Twitter and NOT your web site says that you really value your fans enough to give them something special. Of course, once word gets out that you have a new song available for download, your non-Twittering fans will download it, but your Twitter followers will feel special because you gave them the heads up first.

Get Instant Feedback

Not sure if that hook you're writing is trash or gold? Post a clip on Twitter and if you have enough followers, you'll get instant feedback in minutes! Jason Calacanis, founder of Weblogs Inc. and Mahalo, uses it to get feedback on new designs for Mahalo. Sure, you could say that the fans should have no impact on the music you make, but if you want, you have an instant focus group that has your best interests at heart, wants you to succeed and would love to have you take their feedback into consideration.

Twitter-Exclusive Contests

This falls along the same lines as taking requests via Twitter, except it's more fun. You could create a contest in which they plug your new song or upcoming show in one of their updates and that enters them into a drawing where the winner gets free tickets to an upcoming show in their area. You get free promotion, they get to come to your show for free and their followers check out your new song. It's a win-win for everyone involved.

This is really just scratching the surface of how musicians can leverage Twitter to build their brand, increase their audience and get more people to hear their music. I'm sure as time goes on and more and more bands adopt Twitter the way they did MySpace, we'll see some really innovative ways to use Twitter, but these ideas should be enough to get you started. Good luck and follow me on Twitter!

Is Twitter For Twits?

I hear it all the time. The people on twitter are twits, twittering tales of hairballs and haircuts. Bloggers have been moaning about the noise on twitter, and predicting the date the site will close down, yet twitter remains a powerful communications force in the online world.

I think it has something to do with that thing they call API...the stuff programmers use to talk to twitter and make other tools that use twitter information for something else. I didn't really understand what use it would be to aggregate all these useless posts, until I noticed that some people are posting really valuable stuff. Like the BBC and CNN! Yes, these news sites twitter their top headlines into their twitter account, for all the world to see.

Now, things like twittervision are interesting, and give you a glimpse of world twitter activity, but it sure can waste time too...kind of like what a twit would do, right?

With a little thoughtfulness, you might be able to imagine twittervision done right - showing only the twitters of your friends or a region. So far, that's not happening. But there are a lot of powerful tools being developed to make twitter more personal and available. Like the SMS integration, which lets you read and respond to twitterings from your cell phone. Or twitterfox, a firefox browser plugin that lets your twitters pop up while you surf. This latter tool is even more powerful now, by filtering the replies from your posts, so you can scroll through the responses from others, and respond to them with one click of the mouse.

Other people are using twitter for business, and developing their reach even further simply by posting some of their work on twitter. Lately, I have found poets, reporters, marketers, CEO's, and others, all focusing their twitters to provide useful content relating to their specialty. It makes me think that soon all the major business communications will be carried over twitter, as a new medium to reach a wider audience.

The beauty of twittering is it is like instant messaging, without being instant. People don't expect an immediate response, don't see if you are online or not, but do get to see your response when you post it, so they can catch up to the conversation when- ever they want to, and respond to things without worrying about the interactive requirements of a phone conversation or instant messaging session (big time wasters in this world of ours).

Still, there are millions of people using twitter, and many of them are twits, twittering about toilets and termites that no one else wants to hear about. I like people who do something to fix this problem, and one free tool is at Quotably, and lets you search twitter and group responses into conversations that you can read and respond to. It's quite powerful when you think about it, and perhaps it will help you to see where twitter might go in the future.

It's an exciting world for the twitterers of today.

Twitter is an Effective Tool for Internet Marketers

What is Twitter? Well, on the Twitter login page it is introduced as: a service for friends, family, and co-workers to communicate and stay connected through the exchange of quick, frequent answers to one simple question: What are you doing?

The concept of Twitter at first glance appears to offer a very unique method of communicating with people for casual banter. However, if you are marketing in any way on the Internet, this can be a powerful platform for providing information and for generating traffic.

When entering a message (known as a Tweet), the user is forced to communicate effectively, because the content is limited to 140 characters. It does not take long to figure out how to concisely get your Tweet across.

If Twitter is new to you, perhaps you have not yet grasped its true potential. It definitely has to be one of the best free traffic generators on the Internet. Its simplicity and accessibility has made this tool extremely attractive to over two million users, and that figure seems to be growing exponentially.

Once you register to participate on Twitter (http://twitter.com), you will begin to follow other Twitterers. But, the real key for you as a marketer is to generate your own followers. Thus, giving you the opportunity to get your message out quickly and easily.

As with any marketing headline, the goal of the Tweet is to capture the reader's attention and lead them to where your moneymaker content is located (sales page, opt-in, article, etc). Within your 140 characters you hopefully entice the reader and provide a short hyperlink.

Beyond the linked message area, the perks of this site are multifaceted. The page begins with an automatic welcome that introduces you to the reader and invites them to become a follower. Next, in a personal information area in the upper right corner of the page you can embed a link to a web page and provide a brief bio.

Of course, if you are going to encourage folks to follow you (or to retain followers), your Tweets need to offer value. For the Internet marketer there can sometimes be a fine line between responsibly leading someone to more information or using a platform to blatantly spam an unwanted message.

Take the opportunity to promote your Twitter page whenever possible. Place your Twitter link on your website, blog, ezine, article signature box, and so on. For example, this is my link: http://twitter.com/davidschaefer, and I encourage you to become a follower.

Twitter.com includes a few more features not mentioned here – just visit the help section. And, everyday creative entrepreneurs are offering new products and services to independently support and expand the use of Twitter. The most important point is to take advantage of Twitters simplicity, effectiveness, and potential marketing reach.

Twitter Blog Traffic-generate Traffic With Twitter

Twitter is in a league of its own, it's a different kind of web 2.0 social marketing. It's nothing like MySpace and Facebook, or even Digg and Propeller to name a few. It's a lot more like blogging and mini-blogging and micro-blogging and yet it's not. So what the heck is Twitter and how do you profit from it?

Twitter is one part chat and one part blogging. Mini blogging to be exact, as you only get 140 characters per post. Some businesses such as traffic generation explosion like to referrer to Twitter as Micro-blobbing.

You can also use Twitter on your cell phone to keep in touch better. Some of the benefits are you have the aspects of social sites because you can follow others and be followed as well.

1. Immediate Interaction

The immediate interaction is one reason to use twitter in your marketing efforts. This will help build the relationship with your customers and friends that so many are looking for.

You get to interact immediately with your customers (followers) in a way you can't do with a regular blog or even via comments on sites like MySpace and Facebook.

2. Twitter is being used by everyone

This goes along with number one. You get closer to your customer base which helps build your relationship. As more and more people start using Twitter you will see more benefits, so will your competition. If you don't adapt and take advantage of applications like Twitter you'll be left behind and lose customers.

3. Short and to The Point, make it count

Twitter like a phone text message, limits you to 140 characters. We all know we are too busy, get bombarded with too many marketing messages and too many emails to read much more than that anyway. Your customers will appreciate these short and to the point messages.

If you're not using Twitter, I highly recommend you start. It's another marketing channel for your Internet marketing efforts to pay off. http://www.traffic-generation-explosion.com would like to thank Twitter for all they do. Keep up the great work Twitter.

Author: Al Ferretti, Jim Grygar, Skeeter Hansen

Using Twitter for Business

When I first heard about Twitter--a tool for instantly broadcasting the stream-of-consciousness minutiae of your life to the world--I was pretty sure it was a cross between a complete waste of time and navel gazing on crack.

Turns out I was right.

A quick peek at the most recent posts--called "tweets"--include information on what people are having for breakfast, laptop woes and depressed thoughts over last night's home team loss. (Plus a bunch of foreign-language tweets that may range from the ridiculous to the sublime and back again.)

Twitter users--often called Tweeple (or worse) can update their status using 140 characters or less, the aforementioned "tweet." If you join Twitter you can "follow" other tweeple, which causes their updates to appear on your home page. In turn, they can follow you as well, a form of permission-based marketing. You can also converse with them through Twitter, but always in 140 characters or less.

It's kind of like an IT haiku.

Within this expanding base of exhibitionist navel gazers are a growing number of people who are using Twitter for business. And I'm not just talking about aggressive Web marketers who tweet every blog post they make and create links to all their online activities.

Rather, there are professionals who are using Twitter as a communications tool. (Imagine that!) Here's how you can use Twitter for business:

* Followindustry leaders who post links to important resources and influence conversations.

* Post questions for quick answers and answer others' questions to establish your credibility and expertise.

* Keep up on the buzz in your industry.

* Network with like-minded people.

To find these interesting tweeple in the midst of all that noise, you can use the Twitter search box that will search matches in others' profiles, but not on individual tweets. Here are a couple of 3rd party tools that allow for more advanced searches:

* Who Should I Follow?: Finds and suggests like-minded people based on your tweets.

* Summize: Allows you to search tweets for keywords and offers lots of customization tools.

The more people who follow you on Twitter, the more influence and networking opportunities you have. Thus, it makes sense to try and build a following. Here are some ideas on getting others to follow you:

* Follow them. There's an almost kneejerk reaction to follow people who follow you.

* Post some good tweets right before following someone else. I find that if someone follows me and they only tweet about how hungry or tired they are, I don't follow them back. The same goes for people who haven't tweeted in a while.

* Reply to people you are following, especially if they're not yet following you. That's a good way to engage someone and get them to follow you, even if they didn't follow you immediately. Remember, though, some people have thousands of followers, and may not be able to respond to every reply.

While the rules and guidelines of Twitter etiquette are still evolving, guidelines from other social media sites can used:

* Treat others with respect

* Participate in the community

* Do more than promote your own agenda.

Professionals and consultants have had the most impact at Twitter; most businesses are still trying to figure out how to use Twitter as a communications tool. If you're not a one-person shop, here are a few ideas to help get your creative juices flowing:

* A restaurant tweets their daily specials

* A ticket agency tweets about-to-expire tickets

* A realtor tweets new homes on the market

* A chamber of commerce tweets local events and promotions.

For more ideas, or just to engage me in conversation, I invite you to follow me at Twitter. I promise not to tell you what I had for lunch.
Unless it's really good.

Building Online Community Using Twitter

Have an online community is must for online business. Without strong community, it can hard for you to sell anything. However, community building is not as easy as we thought. You have to work us to build it.

There is couple way to build online community. And twitter is the fast way to start it if you like to start your own online community. Twitter can give you head to head information for everyone who follows your twitter.

For start, you have to follow couple of people. Yes, you have followed them first. Maybe for start you must follow at least 50 people. Then, make sure you add your twitter in your blog. It can make you closer with your visitor. They can feel save with you because they know you and they know what you do.

To add twitter in your blog is very easy. You only have to http://twitter.com/badges/. Choose which badges that you want to add. I love HTML & JavaScript Badge. It is full customized. In the bottom of your twitter, you can add your twitter page.

Well, the end part of twitter building community, you have always update your twitter. As long as you online, keep update it. It only few word. I know you can do it easily. However, if your community has built already, you can start to promote your business. However keep it like recommendation not promotion.

At the end part of this article, if you like to follow my twitter, you can free follow me on http://twitter.com/qzoners. Well, keep update with my next article. Hope you like it. And please leave me a comment for better article.

A Clean Twitter Is A Good Twitter

Twitter has been called micro-blogging, or blogging for ordinary people. Basically they have provided a way for people who don't want a fully fledged blog to post about their daily happenings.

The downside to Twitter is the amount of people who sign up and make a post, but then never return. Currently these abandoned accounts are never deleted, so it's up to you to update your follower and following lists keeping them clear of these abandoned accounts.

Finding Followers:

Besides being able to add your friends and email contacts to Twitter, they also provide a handy search box to help you find people to follow.

One of the best ways to get followers is to follow others first,. There is one check you must do before adding someone to your list, the most recent post date. Just adding thousands of people to your twitter list will not bring you followers. Twitter received a lot of buzz and attracted a lot of tire kickers, but if you aren't paying attention then you could easily end up with the majority of your list being people who haven't logged on to Twitter for a months, and they won't be coming back to check out your profile anytime soon.

So step one to a clutter-free Twitter is to follow the right people. I will search for a particular term, and flip through the list, signing up to follow only people who have posted in the last 7 days. Also I will not follow anyone on their first post, I want to make sure they will be coming back on a regular basis.

Culling The List:

As your lists grow, you will want to check your following list and un-check those who have not posted for a while. I like to use a 30 day rule. Every time I log on to Twitter, I check 5 to 10 people in my list, and stop following the ones who have not made a post in the last 30 days. Many people don't post every day, or even every week, but chances are if they have not posted in the last month, they probably won't be posting again.

Following Followers:

Step 3 is returning the favor. Whenever you log in, check your follower list to make sure you are returning the favor to everyone that is following you. Unless they are just spamming the Twitter system with affiliate links posted every couple of minutes, there is no reason not to give back.

Posting With Links:

When writing a post with a link, whether to your site, an affiliate link, or just something cool you found, there is no need to place a full URL. Just using the www.sitename.com format will automatically make a clickable link.

While affiliate links are okay, try to post valuable content as well. Just putting up a bunch of obvious affiliate links will lose your following.

5 Tips for Using Twitter in a Generous Way

Apart from having Ezines and Wordpress automatically feed Twitter, there are various ways you can focus on giving to others with it. I have created a list of 5 things that give you the satisfaction of sharing with others useful information on Twitter, instead of rambling on about how "ticked off I am that it is raining"-useless information! I am not condemning fun on Twitter. However if you are following 10 people, and one of them just focuses on personal expressions like the one above, chances are you expect their future tweets less worthwhile.

1.   Offer a Free Report

To do this you will need a File-Transfer-Protocol so you can upload a PDF of something you want to share. Sometimes you will find it already online, in which case you can just give the link through twitter.

2.   Give people news/link to something you found that was particularly helpful to you.

I recently added names like Timothy Ferriss and Steve Pavlina. These guys do this all the time. They will link to a website that helped them or complements the content on their blog.

3.   Promote your blog.

Of course this is being generous. You just want to hone in on Twitter WIIFM (What's In It For Me?). Put your topic in a broad light and post it on Twitter with a URL. Twitter allows you to "mini-blog," which means you can explore a slightly different title through it to attract visitors to your site.

4. YouTube

This one is a no brainer. Video information is being trans-
ferred between people at an alarmingly high rate. A website that
does not have some kind of movies is being ignorant of a high
percentage of its visitors who may not want to read pages and
pages of information.

5. Announce your presence

Making face on through various events is important. Don't
be a faceless blogger who never shows up in public. Create free
speaking events or just an event for coffee reserved for your readers. I understand websites and blogs are global, however there
could be people who are in town and would like to meet you.

And that's it really. What you want to do is create anticipa-
tion from your follows so that you keep going back for more
updates.

Live for something!

Using Facebook And Twitter To Market Your Ebook And Online Business

Social networking has made the process of marketing your eBook much easier. By having a presence on Facebook and Twitter you can position yourself as an expert in your field in a very short time. Even while you are still writing your eBook, get started on these two social media sites and become the go-to person in your niche.

Facebook now has more than one hundred million members, so the best way to let people know about you and your eBook is to start your own group. You can use the title of your eBook as the title of the group you create, provided it is filled with your keywords.

You can invite your Facebook friends to join your group, but people will also be able to find your group by typing your keywords into Google or any other search engine. For example, if you type eBook writing and technology into Google, my Facebook group is number one. How cool is that?

You will also want to create a page on Facebook with the name of the eBook as the title. A page is separate from your profile in that it is specifically about your business or your product, which in this case is your eBook.

This page will also rank high in the search engines, but that is not the only way it will help people to find you and your eBook. When you create a page you can also import your blog's RSS feed into the page. This means that every time you make a post to your blog it will automatically be syndicated into

Facebook. Even though you can do this in other areas of Facebook, being able to import your blog, where you are writing about your niche topic, will give your eBook even more exposure.

My strong recommendation is that you purchase a domain name that is the same as the name of your eBook, and then forward that domain to your page on Facebook. Your blog's domain name can be something very similar, or it can be exactly the same with a different extension. For example, your blog may end with dot come, whereas your Facebook page may end with dot net. This is a great way to take full advantage of your keywords, while branding your name and your niche at the same time.

Twitter is the other major player in the social networking arena. You can set up your account to automatically tweet your blog posts at certain times each day. When you write about your eBook in one of your blog posts, anyone who is following you on Twitter will see what you have written.

Even though you are limited to 140 characters with each tweet, you can shorten your links by using a site such as tinyurl or bitly. This enables you to provide great information about your eBook in the space you are allowed. You may also want to give out a sample chapter to your Twitter followers so that they can see if this is something they will be interested in purchasing. I recommend doing this while you are still writing, so that you will already have prospects when you are ready to make sales.

The combination of Facebook, Twitter, and your blog will give you the online presence you need in order to sell your eBook and become known to your target audience. By seeing your name in so many places, you will be able to attract new prospects and clients on a regular basis.

By getting involved in social networking right now, you will be able to position yourself as the expert in your niche. People will know who you are and associate you with your topic. There has never been a better time to be online than right now, and social networking speeds up the process of building your list and gaining the credibility and visibility necessary to sell your eBook and building your online empire.

Twictionary of Twitter Terms - Part 1

We hear them all the time, terms and slang being bandied about, and many people just nod and smile vacantly, while wondering quietly to themselves "What the Tweet did THAT mean?"

The first in a series of Twictionary tweets aims to shed some light on some of the terms you'll hear and read about Twitter.

Make sure you don't miss part 2 by following me on Twitter!

BARACK OBAMA: Probably the world's most famous Twitterer.

FOLLOW: Choosing to sign up to receive someone's Tweets.

FOLLOW+USER NAME: The instruction to keep up with a user's flow of Twitter messages

FOLLOWERS: People who follow your updates.

GEOTWITTER: Tracks the geographical location of the most recent Tweets.

This service is updated every minute.

GET+USER NAME: A command that retrieves the most recent updated Tweet from that user.

JACK DORSEY: Widely acknowledged as the inventor of Twitter.

JAIKU: A competitor of Twitter, currently owned by Google.

LOUDTWITTER: Automatically transfer your Tweets directly to your blog.

MICRO-BLOG: A tiny way to blog. (Twitter only allows 140 characters)

MISTWEET: A message or 'Tweet' that was sent in error.

NUDGE+USER NAME: A Twitter command used to remind a Friend to update their Twitter status

OBVIOUS: The American company based in California that created Twitter.

POLITWEETS: A tool for tracking Tweets relating to politics

QUOTABLY: Follow the Tweets of a particular user in a threaded style

ReTWEETme: Use Twitter to remind yourself of things you might forget. When the time comes, Twitter will message you the reminder.

RUBY ON RAILS: The programming language used to create and develop Twitter.

SUMMIZE: A tool for searching the content of hundreds of thousands of Tweets.

Part 2 tomorrow!

To find out more about using Twitter for Business, visit www.businessontwitter.co.uk

Tweeting yourself to a Better Career

The convergence of PR and social media is inevitable, and the ways in which those of us in the industry use social media continue to expand. One area that has seen some interesting changes is recruiting, and the role played by social networks. Nearly everyone is familiar with LinkedIn, a very conventional yet very useful tool for both the recruiter and the professional looking to make a career change now, or just interested in building out a network of people in the industry. Facebook, too, which in 2007 opened its doors beyond its college/university roots to professionals is finding increasing adoption among recruiters.

More interesting still is the use of what I would call emerging tools, either newer social networks or social media tools that might not be immediately associated with a career search, but which you might want to look into any way.

Lately, I have been spending a lot more time on Twitter, which can best be described as a global instant messaging system. I won't offer a Twitter tutorial here, but here's the quick downlow on it. Twitter was launched in 2006, and in 2007, after winning a high profile industry award, the service really began to take off and soon became a phenomenon. Twitter comes under a new social media heading called "micro blogging," tools that let you blog simply, quickly, and tersely. Twitter is basically IM, limited to 140 characters. Like most social media, Twitter is free. You sign up, establish an identity and then add people that you are "following" on Twitter. Twitter describes its various features and actions in a very unique way, which might be part of the "bad press" it has received. Your posts are called "updates" or "tweets." You are "following" the people whose updates you add to your "timeline," and the people who add you to their timeline are called "follow-

Page 156

ers." (If you want to see what Twitter looks like in action, just go to the home page and click "Public Timeline.")

For a long time, many people criticized Twitter as an endless stream of narcissistic and mundane chatter. Recently, however, as people have learned to adapt Twitter to more important tasks than communicating that you have just fed your cat, the service has begun to see a number of interesting commercial uses.

Many recruiters are now using Twitter to better connect with candidates. A search on the term "recruit" on Twitter's home page returns 87 people somehow associated with recruiting. (Not all of them are recruiters. Check the user profiles for more information on each person.) Among these is Lindsay Olson, PRJobs on Twitter, a public relations recruiter. I "met" Lindsay through Twitter. I was impressed by how she uses Twitter. Lindsay "converses" with people on Twitter in a very natural way, letting them see the daily worklife of a recruiter. In this way, Lindsay develops credibility, and builds friendships with a large number of candidates and connections to potential candidates.

I interviewed Lindsay by email on how she uses Twitter. She confirmed my view, which is that any "commercial" use of social media requires an understanding of the etiquette and unique attributes of the medium, and a willingness to downplay hype and conventional marketing tactics:

"As a recruiter and business professional utilizing social media technologies in my business, I think the single most important way of communicating this way is by joining the conversation as a peer, and interacting on a personal level. If you are just throwing links to your jobs and your business out there, your followers get sick of the shameless self-promotion. I think the day in the life of a recruiter is somewhat of a mystery to many people, especially potential candidates, and have found Twitter to be an excellent tool to share my profession. I feel that sharing my successes, failures and experiences in recruiting is helpful for people to understanding how to better interact with a recruiter as well as potential hiring companies."

Many recruiters, and business people in general, have been reluctant to use social networks for commercial purposes due to privacy concerns. In fact, I contacted one recruiter, who uses Facebook and LinkedIn but not Twitter, and she agreed to speak with me for this piece, but only as an unidentified background source.

I asked Lindsay about this and she said that it is not "a concern as long as our clients' and candidates' confidentiality is respected in public," which she makes a part of the rules she holds herself to in her use of all social media.

I strongly recommend looking into Twitter and other "alternative" social media as part of your career networking plan. The world of Web 2.0 -- blogs, podcasts, wikis, social networks, etc. -- is a highly connected and visible one. This high visibility environment has its etiquette, and brings with it the learning curve of any new technology, but the rewards of being so visible and so well connected to the right people can far outweigh the effort required to get up to speed.

15 Tweets of Fame

Fake celebrity bloggers and Twitterers. They're the cubic zirconiums of social media. They aren't real, but in some ways, they shine brighter than the genuine object, and they can't help but catch our eye.

The craze started in the blogosphere. Last year's most talked about CEO blog wasn't written by a CEO at all. The Fake Steve Jobs blog, which turned out to have been written by Forbes reporter Dan Lyons, was the subject of constant buzz, not only as people speculated as to who was actually writing it, with some suspecting ironically that it might have been written by Jobs himself, but also as we got to read a pretty good interpretation of what Jobs might have said, were he not such a secretive CEO.

I was asked by the Christian Science Monitor why I thought fake CEO blogs were so popular, and I felt it was because "parody is a good way to touch a figure that doesn't want (to) – or can't take the time to – be bothered with honest and direct communication." The fake celebrity craze has made its way to Twitter. There are lots of celebrities on Twitter, more of them bogus than authentic. Whenever a celebrity turns up on Twitter, there's all kinds of excitement as the news spreads through the network, and then, more often than not, there's the second round of news in which the fraud is uncovered.

In February, author Seth Godin disappointed thousands when he revealed that not only was the Seth Godin on Twitter bogus, but the real Seth Godin did not have time to be on Twitter.

But there are real Twitter celebrities. If you'd like, treat the following list as a quiz, and visit the Twitter profile for each person to see if you can figure out which ones are real, and which are the creations of fans.

Henry Rollins
MC Hammer
Richard Dawkins
Stephen Colbert or Stephen Colbert or Stephen Colbert
Chuck Norris
David Letterman
Bill Gates
Borat
William Shatner
Snoop Dogg
50 Cent

(Go to original article for Twitter links)

Henry Rollins, MC Hammer, Snoop Dogg and 50 Cent are the genuine article, so far. (And I have my doubts about fitty.) If you're on Twitter, you can add them as friends and maybe even engage them in conversation. And even some of the real ones may turn out to be inauthentic. (I have to add this disclaimer as many of the pretenders, Seth Godin for example, and Richard Dawkins, were at times VERY GOOD at their impersonations, fooling all of the people all of the time, for a time.)

The others are frauds. (Many of the bogus celebrity names are in use by more than one user.) Most were either outed by other Twitter users, or simply confessed. A fake Stephen Colbert said "Shall I continue this farce or retire the account?" Or maybe fraud isn't the word. Maybe they're online performance artists. Or maybe they're filling a need we have to know celebrities one-on-one. Plenty of people defend the practice, likening it to a similar custom in the past of using celebrity names in chat rooms, but the difference is, there was no expectation pre Web 2.0 you were actually chatting with Angelina Jolie or Vlad the Impaler.

What do you think? Is there anything wrong with someone impersonating a celebrity on Twitter as long as they don't do it to damage someone's reputation or to misappropriate money? Is it just "good fun" or is it deceptive? What does the practice do for the state of trust in our social networks?

And please add me on Twitter. I promise I'm for real.

Also check out Talent Zoo on Twitter!

Social Networking: Quality Vs. Quantity

The value of your social networks is largely based on the quality, and to some extent quantity, of people in them.

While nearly all social networks have a "Terms of Service" (TOS), the rules for participation (don't post obscenities or copyrighted material, for example), the etiquette for adding people to each network is defined by the mores of those on the network. It's also highly subject to change when early adopters (who tend to be purists) become outnumbered by "newcomers."

When developing your strategy for adding people, you'll want to consider who you are and why you're on the network. For this column I am assuming predominantly professional use. Although I'm focusing on LinkedIn, Facebook and Twitter for this article, the same concepts apply to many other networks.

Some choose to connect with very few people, often confining their social networking to people they already know through other means. My strategy is what some people refer to as "promiscuous." I will accept an invitation from nearly anyone, to connect on any network, because I am a social media professional interested in the efficiency and velocity of new media tools, and I want to be completely open minded about who I connect with in order to be open to new learning experiences and diverse viewpoints. You'll need to figure out what's comfortable for you.

General Advice

* Connect with people with like experience and interests, the same schools and employers, or those who are potential mentors.

* Know and follow the rules (aka TOS) of the network you are on.

* Obvious attempts to curry favor with potential employers are just that.

* Male users should be particularly careful to avoid the appearance of flirtation and inappropriate comments and messages. Sure, it happens in the other direction, but not much. Use the same rules as you would in the workplace.

* Don't send blatantly commercial messages. Business networking is OK. Shameless promotion and cold calling is not.

* If the network allows, give the person you are inviting some context for the invitation.

* Err on the side of conservatism. If in doubt about the appropriateness of connecting with someone, hold off.

* Be willing to give and get. Think beyond what is "in it for you."

* Don't add connections simply to display an impressive number. Quality trumps quantity. As my friend Ophelia says, "Connect, don't collect."

* Don't worry about having only a few connections if you're new. Your network will grow as the value you offer others becomes apparent.

* Be modest about the number of connections you have.

* Do not take it badly if someone declines or ignores your invitation to connect. That's their option.

* Many people will decline all unexpected invites. In some cases, you can inform them ahead of time you want to invite them, increasing your odds of acceptance.

Each network has slightly different protocol for adding connections. Here are my experiences and thoughts on each.

LinkedIn

LinkedIn is the oldest, most established and most traditional of these three networks. LinkedIn also has the most controls over who can connect with who, and the severest penalties for failing to follow these rules. LinkedIn is generally a network for career and business development, and is structured to ensure that members create trusted networks of connections with like interests who already know each other in some way.

LinkedIn validates each request you make for an introduction by requiring you to document how you know the person you are connecting with, and actively recommends you do not connect with people you don't know. If the person is not in your immediate circle, you may have to go through one or more intermediaries for an introduction.

Recently, a number of people have found a "workaround" in LinkedIn that lets you add almost anyone by creating a new "Group" or "Association" with nearly any name, like "Blog" or "Twitter" or "Blogosphere."

LinkedIn has also spawned a number of "communities," like LinkedIn LIONS and MyLink500.com, dedicated to helping people add large volumes of connections.

When extending a LinkedIn invitation, you should add to the standard message that LinkedIn sends by adding a personal message explaining to the recipient why you are contacting them.

LinkedIn also maintains a strict policy on "I Don't Knows," popularly known as IDKs. If you send an invite to a user who does not know you, and they reply "I Do Not Know this person," that is a point against you, and if you get five IDKs, you can be booted from the network.

Facebook

Facebook has a fairly advanced search tool for finding new connections (and like most networks, tools for adding people from other networks, or using your email address book to find people). You can use Facebook's networks or browse friends of friends to see former co-workers and classmates you can connect with. It's also easy to find people in your industry.

When you send an invite to someone to connect on Face-book, you can "add a personal message" to your invite. If you are not previously acquainted but feel this person is appropriate to connect with, this is a good place to type something like "I really enjoy your blog" or "Would love to connect to talk about (insert subject here)." This will greatly increase the odds for acceptance.

When you invite someone on Facebook, they will be able to see your profile, so if your information is up to date, they will be able to make a decision based on your experience, age, gender, etc.

I find the etiquette on Facebook in general to be a little overwhelming and confusing, possibly due to the network's early roots among students. For example, the "poke" was originally a suggestive gesture meant to indicate that you were interested in hooking up with the person you poked. Some people now use a poke simply to say "hey!" Women in particular HATE getting a Facebook poke from anyone but a boyfriend or spouse, so be very careful.

Twitter

Adding connections on Twitter is expressed in terms of "Following" and "Followers." You can see the updates (posts) of the people you follow and the people following you can see your updates. Twitter is very transparent in showing how many of each you have. Opinion varies widely on this point, but I think a balanced number is good. It's not perfectly valid as a statistical indicator, but at least suggests that you are interested in the conversational aspect of the network. I think having too many followers vs. following is indicative of an inflated sense of self and a touch of narcissism.

Women on Twitter are very wary of male users who are only following 600 female users in their teens and 20s. This kind of profile makes a guy look like a stalker, and then again, if this is your profile, you are one. There are currently grassroots efforts to indentify and ban these people, which I think is a bit much, but this kind of behavior is not appropriate on any general purpose social network.

Finding and adding is simple. Search for new connections using the "Find Folks" box on the right sidebar. Twitter's search tool is very unsophisticated. I use the following terms for finding people in my profession: media, social, PR, public relations, communications. You can follow anyone by clicking on their "handle" (Twitter name) to follow them. They may or may not follow you back.

On Twitter, I will follow back anyone who follows me unless they are:

* A bot that is designed to send me marketing messages

* Someone who sends obscene, racist or otherwise inappropriate material (you can check this by looking at their previous updates)

* Someone with no profile whatsoever

Some people "protect" their updates, which means you can request to follow them through the process outlined above, but they must approve your request. Personally, I do not protect my updates, but I guess people have reasons for doing so. Conversely, you can block specific users whom you do not want seeing your updates.

General Courtesy

I always thank people both for inviting me, and for accepting my invitations, on Twitter and sometimes on Facebook and LinkedIn. (Twitter is more suited to such informal communication.)

Of course, as I mentioned, etiquette is ever changing and also very personal. This is my take on these three popular networks. Your results may vary. Etiquette is also wrapped up in the functionality of each network, so you have to know the interface and how to connect before you can do it without offending.

This piece is quite a bit longer than I generally write, but I've barely covered the subject. Please comment below or email me with your reactions and experiences, And add me to Facebook, Twitter and LinkedIn if you'd likc!

Social Networking for Businesses

Social networking - the phrase is everywhere these days. Blogs this. MySpace that. These new technologies have revolutionized the way we function in the 21st century. But what can they do for you and your business? A lot, actually. These sites involve way more than posting pictures online and sending messages to your friends. Online social networking sites exist purely to build relationships and in the business world this is a very important thing. If you're looking for a way to build up relationships with other businesses or to reach out to clients, this is definitely the new age way to go.

Popular online social networking tools include blogs, MySpace.com, Facebook.com and Twitter.com. All offering distinct and different features, it's up to you to decide which will be best for your business networking needs. Below is a summary of each of these networking tools and how they can get you connected to clients, customers and other businesses.

Blogs
Blogs (the collaboration of 'web log') have been around since the early 1990s and have continued to grow in popularity since. In December 2007 it was reported by blog search engine site, Technorati, that there were 112 million blogs out there in cyberspace. Blogs are a great way to let the world know what you're all about. You can write anything you want in your blog. It's also a good way to get feedback, as others are able to comment on what you have written. Google also loves blogs, so your blog is likely to be picked up by the search engine through the use of keywords. That's more exposure for your business and it's absolutely free.

A handy aspect of the blog for business networking is the blogroll. A blogroll is a list of affiliated sites that appears in your blog's sidebar. Viewers of your blog can see whom you're associated with and who is associated with you. This helps you build up reputation, credibility and authenticity.

So how do you become a blogger? It's easy. There are two ways you can do this.

1. Sign up to a site such as blogger.com, LiveJournal.com or WordPress.com. Set up account and the hard work is done for you. Just type away, hit publish and your message will instantly be out there.

2. Get a blog incorporated into your existing site. This is the more professional approach, and it will assist in getting potential clients or customers back onto your website if you update frequently.

PROS: easy to use, great exposure through search engines and they're an extremely popular mode of communication at present

CONS: need frequent updating if they are to be successful

MySpace.com
This site is extremely popular. Launched in 2003, MySpace.com allegedly has over 100 million accounts registered to it. The site itself has a wide variety of features that can help with business networking. MySpace.com is also a great way to gain exposure as profiles can be made to be highly public - to view someone's page you do not have to be registered with the site.

For business purposes, the following are features that prove useful in creating and maintaining networks and relationships with allies and customers.

'Top Friends': here is where you rank your friends. It's a good space to show who you're affiliated with - hopefully they will return the favor and will be promoting you on their page as well!

Bulletins: posting a bulletin sends a message to everyone on your friends list. It's a quick and simple way to get a message out there.

Groups: joining a group gives you a common page with others in the group. It's another way of showing whom you're associated with, where you're employed, or what your interests are.

PROS: lots of active users, interactive

CONS: large following of teenagers using it for solely social purposes

Facebook.com

Often regarded as the grown-ups MySpace.com, Facebook.com has been around since 2004 but gained prominence in 2006 when it became available to everyone over the age of 13. Facebook.com is especially known for its networking features. Belonging to certain networks and groups is an important aspect of Facebook.com. Users can choose to belong to one main network (such as their company or university network) and those who belong to that network can see their profile. It's a good way of building contacts in your chosen industry and keeping in touch with those from work. Other useful features include:

Groups: users can belong to multiple groups, and the groups you belong to shows up on your profile's sidebar.

The Wall: allows you to post messages to those on your friends list or in your network.

Status: updating this shows users on your friends list or network what you are doing - a great way to tell everyone that you're working hard!

Facebook.com also has a News Feed which alerts you as to what's going on with your friends, upcoming events and profile changes.

PROS: dedicated to networking, more mature users, usability is good

CONS: high levels of privacy - you need to be friends with people or in their network to view their information (although there are options to make your information more public)

Twitter.com

Twitter.com is a relatively new social networking site that was established in 2006. It differs from MySpace.com and Facebook.com as it is a purely text-based medium. With Twitter.com, you post short messages to your page (up to 140 characters) to alert others, who are 'following' you, of what you are doing or where you are...or anything you want. Twitter.com has a simple search option so it is easy to find people you know or businesses that you want to see updates from. Like the other sites, this is another way of linking yourself to other people, businesses or organization. It helps to establish connections. People are generally interested in other people, so let clients and associated businesses know what you're up to - it will create personality for your business and strengthen relationships.

PROS: it is simple and doesn't have redundant features for business networking. Twitter.com also branches out - you can access it from your mobile, software on your browser or through instant message

CONS: not as well-known as other social networking sites

Embracing social networking technology

Go on, give it a try. By embracing this communication technology you are essentially deepening links between you and other businesses, and promoting yourself to clients and potential customers. Don't underestimate the power of the Internet - make a name for your business on it and you will reap the rewards. Business networking is key to a successful business so get out there and let the world know what you're all about.

The Future of Communications: are You in or are You Out?

Recently I've been spending time on Twitter, and Plurk as I continue to explore social media. As I invite friends and colleagues to join me using these tools, I often have to defend the time I'm spending—some would argue wasting—at these sites.

Here's why I do it: tools like Twitter and Plurk represent the future of communications.

I'm not arguing that anyone will be using or even talking about Twitter or Plurk a few years from now. But they represent a newmanner of communication that will become more relevant, more important as people join in and feed this emerging network of social media communications.

There are a number of reasons why this is happening.

Short Attention Spans. One catalyst is that we live in a culture where ADD is now considered a coping mechanism for dealing with the constant barrage of information we face.

This is characterized by political sound bites, lead news stories that clock in at ninety seconds, and commercials optimized for TiVo fast-forwarding. Social media communications are likewise short and chaotic; threads/messages are started and dropped with little warning, and are often limited to 140 characters or less. That means the previous sentence is 22 characters too long for either a Tweet or a Plurk.

A New Definition of Privacy. Right or wrong, in a post 9/11 world we've sacrificed many personal rights for the hope of increased security. Cameras at intersections, Real ID cards, and even Fast Lanetransponders that allow us to avoid stopping at toll booths all chip away at our ability to stay under the radar. We're used to being watched. Social media communications are by definition social, and regularly public.

A Desire for Fame and Stature. As Napoleon Bonaparte said, "I have made the most wonderful discovery, I have discovered men will risk their lives, even die, for ribbons!" Fame and stature can be quickly—and less dangerously—achieved in our YouTube/Reality TV/MySpace world.

All successful social networks have a built-in reward system that reflects your standing in the community. For Twitter, it's your number of followers; LinkedIn counts your connections; Plurk's karma point system gives you new icons—ribbons, if you will—for posting more often and inviting new people to Plurk.

There are other factors as well that are changing the way we communicate.

* The desire to be connected at all times, whether through a computer or a mobile device, or something else in the future.

* The high cost of travel that will cut down on face-to-face meetings.

* The increased affordability, quality and functionality of digital communication tools.

I don't see these trends changing drastically in the next few years. We'll continue to be wired, gas prices will continue to rise and we'll continue to want to communicate and network with the other humans on our planet.

Social media represents a major shift in the way we communicate with each other. Not everyone will adapt, but the younger generation is already comfortable with these tools. While there will always be the telephone and email for us "old folks," a lot of important conversations will be going on exclusively in the social media arena.

So I ask you again: The future of communications: are you in, or are you out?

Five Ways You Can Build Your Reputation With Social Networking

Five Ways You Can Build Your Reputation With Social Networking
By Bob Jenkins

Are you using social networks to build your reputation online? Whether you already are or you are just getting started with sites like Twitter, Facebook, and Ning, building your online reputation is your biggest responsibility.

Here are five ways to make sure you do it right.

#1: Be Proud Of Being You

The first thing is, you have to be yourself. You have to be who you are. Because although you can get away with being fake for a little while, as soon as one person realizes that you're not who you say you are, your reputation is destroyed almost instantly because of the power of social networking.

So be yourself. And don't be afraid of being yourself. Realize that you have some gifts and some knowledge that people need to know about, and those that want to learn from you are going to gravitate towards you. Those that don't think you're worth listening to are basically going to ignore you. And it's at their peril, so don't worry about them.

#2: Transparency - Never Hide From Your Audience

The second thing about your reputation is you should try to be transparent at all times. This means you keep everything real with your audience.

For example, over the last year, I used social media to show you my move from Maryland to North Carolina, including drama with the movers, picking the house, and getting it set up. I also pulled back the curtain to show what it takes to run a product launch.

When I did my last product launch, I was Twittering every day what I was doing to get ready for this site. Most of the gurus out there would keep everything under lock and key, and I was being very clear, saying, "This is what I'm doing to get ready for this launch." It actually helped me have a better launch, even though I told everybody exactly what I was going to be doing.

They didn't think that they had some surprise or whatever like most people teach; they just were excited to be part of it and part of the story. So be transparent. Let people know what you're doing and why you're doing it, and they're going to learn how to trust you.

#3: Be Positive For Positive Results

The third way to build your reputation is to be positive.

There are folks out there who generally can do a good job of being negative. I don't know about you, but I don't find that to be a very long-term profitable strategy.

It may get you some attention at first and spark some controversy, but that's not the way to go. Be looking forward to the optimistic of your industry, of your business and what the results are going to be.

It would be easy for you to go onto Twitter or onto Facebook and talk about how you're having a bad day or this product sucks or this week sucks or this relationship sucks. But you're not really there for a support network, per se.

You'll find some of that. If you have something bad happen in your life, sharing it with your followers will be very therapeutic for you and you will get a lot of support back. But when you're just blasting negative things out, you're going to get negative things in return, usually.

So try to be positive as much as possible and look for the opportunities that are out there and look at them from that positive perspective.

#4: Build Your Reputation And They Will Come

The fourth thing you must do is to be patient. This is because, initially, your reputation is going to be built only by yourself and the first initial people who get to know you. But as time goes on and you get more followers and you build a larger network of friends and peers, your reputation will solidify to allow your business to grow.

Once it hits a tipping point, your reputation and business accelerates at a very quick pace.

So be patient and let it happen. Don't try this stuff out for a week and then come back to me next week and say, "Well, it didn't really work. I didn't really get any results yet." You've got to let social networking play out over a few weeks and then a couple months and so on. A year from now your business is going to be tremendously different compared to where it is right now.

#5: Contribute To The Conversation – Every Day!

The fifth thing about your reputation is you need to be someone that people look to as a contributor, not as a leech, not as a mooch, as a contributor.

You have to be willing to be involved in the conversation, and you have to be willing to give as much or even more than what you're going to get in return. The people who do that are growing so fast it makes my head spin.

I feel that I'm a pretty giving person but I see some other folks out there that just keep on giving, giving, giving and they just build up a huge following and that social capital is a real asset to your business. So you need to make sure that you're contributing as much as possible to the conversation.

I don't mean that as just go around randomly and try to help people. Within your specific task, your specific industry, the things you know well, you need to be at the forefront of letting people know how to do what you know how to do without charging them money at first.

They'll come and find your site and your products and they'll pay you for that as time goes on and their needs grow. With social networking you need to be building your reputation up first.

If somebody has a question, you should be one of the first people who answers and you need to answer without reservation not just, "Oh, I answered that in my eBook; go buy it". They're going to find your eBook if you just talk to them and give them solutions to the problem they are struggling with at that moment.

Give people your input, your encouragement for them to get better at what they are trying to do.

Any little quick free advice you can give, give it.

Actively Build Your Reputation With Social Networking And Reap The Rewards

You've got to be in this for the reason of having fun and really building that relationship. Dollars will come, there's no doubt about that. But first, connect with people and really help them out. Understand that they'll become loyal followers of what you do and see you for who you are.

Follow these 5 steps to building your reputation online and you'll not only beat your competition, you'll have more fun doing it!

Bob Jenkins teaches business owners how to use internet marketing strategies effectively to attract more customers and get more sales without spending a fortune on advertising. Get more free social networking lessons at www.DiscoverSocialNetworking.com

10 Tips to Increase Blog Traffic

By Aaron Lee

Traffic is the soul to any online business, including the recent trend, the blogs. If you imagine it this way:

You have a business in a mall. Customers find information about your business through coupons. Customers come to the mall and go into your business. They look around and decide if they should purchase or not.

The concept is the same with any online business.

You have a website. Visitors (traffic) find information about your website through advertisements. Visitors search on search engines, find your website and click to your website. They look around and decide if they should purchase or not.

If you compare two together:

Online Business vs. Offline Business

Traffic = Customers

Online Ads = Coupons

Search Engines = Mall

Website = Storefront

No traffic to a website is the same as no customers coming into the mall.

No traffic / No Customers = No Sales in both cases.

Blog-driven websites are becoming more and more popular. If you have a blog, pay attention to the tips below: (not in particular order)

1. Choosing the right platform, domain, and internal tagging (categories) CMS (short for Content Management System) is a computer application used to create, edit, manage, and publish content in a consistently organized fasion. A Blog is a CMS application. The right blog software can make a huge difference. If you use blogger or wordpress templates, make sure they are designed with search engine optimized in mind.

Domain should be carefully thought through before going for it. A domain is not just an URL. A domain represents your brand! It should be unique and easy for people to mention to each other. Don't make it too hard to pronounce. Ideally a domain should have the most important keyword about your business in it, and it should be no longer than 20 characters. You should also always aim for dotcom domains first, simply because "dotcom" is more well known compared to dotnet, dotorg...etc.

Proper internal tagging is very important for both search engines and users. Internal tagging enables search engines to better crawl the various content within your website. Internal tagging also allows users to navigate your website a lot easier, as they can just choose and display certain categories of their interest.

2. Write Title Tags and Content with both Search Engine and Visitors in mind Search Engine is all about relevancy. The more targeted keywords you have in your content the higher you will rank in search engine results for these targeted keywords. Title tags and content should have your targeted keywords in them. The more the better, but avoid spamming. This is why you should also write with visitors in mind. If you mention too much of the same words, it's actually quite annoying. Write with honesty and provide quality content to the best of your ability.

3. Proper bolding and underlying Your writing has to please your readers. Don't make your font too small to read. Use proper bolding and underlying to help readers read more efficiently.

4. Use more than just Text This is self-explanatory. You will see popular blogs or websites make good use of graphics, audios, and videos, just to remove the boredom of plain text.

5. Pay attention to your site stats and focus on topics that's popular and needs attention If you pay attention to the traffic logs of your site, you will be able to tell which posts and topics that your audiences like the best. If you find posts and topics that draw the most traffic, they are probably what people are looking for. If you focus on these topics you will be fulfilling people's needs, thus, increasing your readership and building your authority in these topics. Of course if would be even better if these topics lie around your targeted keywords.

6. Invite Guest Bloggers / Posts It's a good practice to invite guest bloggers to post on your blogs. This will improve the variety of the content on your site. Of course, these guest posts should be relevant to your site.

7. Implement Search Feature I can't tell you how important the search box feature is to a website, especially for blogs with hundreds of archived posts. These archived posts may still be valuable to your visitors. By implementing a search feature on your website you are connecting related content with respect to your visitors' demands / needs.

8. Participate in Social Media, Forums, Blogs and Article Directories Most social media, such as Facebook and Twitter, can allow you to automatically update content to your profile with your blog's RSS / Atom feeds. These Social Media, if used properly, can bring you tremendous amount of traffic.

Participating in forums and blogs related to your niche will help building up your authority and your voice in your niche. Not only that, you will also get backlinks to your website if you have your website URL in your signature. Also, a lot of people on these forums and blogs will click on your signature URL out of curiosity. Same effects can be achieved with submitting articles to article directories.

9. Include Keywords in your Links A lot of people only include their direct website URLs in their links. This is a simple mistake that most people make which dramatically reduces the quality of their backlinks. As previously mentioned, search engines are all about relevancy. The quality of a backlink depends on the relevancy between the linking text of the backlink, the title and the content of the website. If your website is about travel (targeted keyword), make sure the keyword "travel" is mentioned in the linking text.

10. Building your Brand Your brand is like the purpose of your blog. Your readers share the same purpose as you and their loyalty are built based on their level of comfort with your brand. Sticking to your brand is very important as you will be consistently building up your authority and voice within your brand, your community. Your readers follow your brand, and you want loyal, quality, and focused readers.

You can, of course, diversify your website but it takes a lot more work and dedication to build up authority in multiple areas. It also takes a lot of work from the search engine optimization point of view since the relevancy of all the content on your website dramatically changes.

If you already have a solid readers to your existing brand, introducing a completely new subject can be off putting for them.

About the Author

Aaron Lee
Business Growth Strategist
The Entrepreneur Journey of a Business Minder

5 Useful Tips To Make Money Blogging With Food Reviews And Ratings

By Blogger Of The Web Dot Com

Most bloggers love to make money blogging about how to make money online. The interest of blogging has come at a stage where people would blog for anything that concerns about money (example, loan, insurance, credit card) than anything else. Today, I am going to turn the table around and share with you how to blog about food and make money at the same time. Sounds impossible? Read on then.

Most food lovers would usually be interested in food recipes and food reviews. Hence if you focus and write about them well, you can expect some good readership and followers for your blog.

Food Reviews Or Food Recipes?

If you have a great recipe to share, why not just write a blog post on it and share with your fellow readers. However, I would not suggest that you copy a recipe from somewhere and post it, or create a recipe out of your own when you have never try the food yourself. You may drive your readers away consequently. Hence, I would not encourage you to write about food recipes unless you are pretty sure of what you desire to share.

Assuming that you are a food lover, food reviews would be an easier choice and more popular approach since most people love to eat and keen to know where they can find the best food in town. Below are 5 useful tips that you may follow to make money blogging about food (particularly reviews and ratings).

1. Take Good Food Display Photos When Served

Food lovers usually love to see nice photos on the food display when served, follows by the food reviews itself. Food photos taken in very bad environment (eg. poor lighting) would require some Photo-shop skills to "touch up" the photo so that it looks nice and appealing to your readers. With these skills, you will be able to display "mouth-watering" photos to accompany your reviews. Great isn't it? :)

2. Add Your Profile If You Are A Popular Food Reviewer

If you are a well-known and popular food reviewer, why not add your profile to the homepage of your blog and give yourself an introduction? This would add credential to your blog and your reviews would naturally attract tons of readers due to your influence and popularity.

3. Provide Honest Food Ratings And Reviews

Apart from appealing photos, food lovers love to see ratings and reviews too. Give yourself a range eg. out of 5 stars on how you would rate the food that you have tried. Write your most honest review in short paragraphs. Do not always give nice reviews, remember to mention the bad points too. However, you should always support your criticism with facts.

Tip: Remember! Your first food review is crucial to the success of your food review blog. Be more descriptive and always share your taste well.

4. Keep Your Readers Coming Back. Gather Your Supporters!

Your reader today might be gone for tomorrow. So how to keep them coming back? Well, apart from providing regular food reviews, provide means for them to return too. First, setup an RSS Feed for them to subscribe to your blog just like mine "Subscribe To My RSS". Whenever you post a new review, they will be notified and read in their own RSS reader. Another way is to create a

Twitter account like what I did so that they can be your "follower" and get updates whenever you are reviewing food again.

5. Monetize Your Blog With Adsense

Fastest and easiest way to monetize your blog is to add in Google Adsense ads. Adsense is the best pay-per-click advertising program so far as it rewards well and display ads that are most relevant to your blog content (food reviews). Competitive key-words like "food reviews" or "Spanish Food" will drive tons of visitors to your blog if you work on your SEO well.

About the Author

5 Useful Tips To Make Money Blogging With Food Reviews And Ratings | Make Money Blogging With Free Blogging Tips

Are Your Online Marketing Methods Boring? Try Twitter!

By Steve Weber

The most Internet marketing fun you will ever have!

I have to admit there are many parts of Internet marketing which are downright boring for me. Rewriting articles into original content, submitting links to directories, the record keeping involved...these are all important, but they are not my most enjoyable tasks.

Therefore, I am very excited when something comes along which not only works well, but I can have fun with too! Twitter is my cool new Internet marketing tool I have been using lately. I can honestly say it is probably the most fun I have had with any marketing method!

I had my account for a while before I took Twitter serious. Sure it was fun. But was it really worth my time? When I kept seeing many of the top Internet marketing gurus using Twitter, I decided to take a closer look. After all, those top marketers probably weren't spending their time with Twitter unless it was producing results for them.

I decided to give Twitter a closer look. I dug into it to find out exactly how marketers like John Reese and Willie Crawford were using it. It amazed me how much time they were devoting to this new marketing method! My methods were hit and miss at first, but thanks to a few Twitter mentors I was able to craft a system which is working very well for building a large following. At the time of this writing, I am consistently adding more than 50 new followers a day!

Imagine! 50 new leads a day which cost me virtually NOTHING but a small amount of "fun time" on Twitter. Also, the best part about my methods is that the new followers I get are targeted. It really does no good for me to get leads who are not interested in Internet marketing. For example, those tweeting about "gardening" or "coin collecting" really won't do many any good as followers.

Although there are large amounts of Twitter users in the area of Internet marketing, Twitter is also used by followers in many other niches. Once you learn the process of "Twittering" and how to attract targeted followers for your niche, the sky really is the limit! Best of all, unlike many other marketing methods, Twittering is an absolute blast of fun!

Here are a few hints for Twittering success:

- Always have a descriptive bio of yourself and include a great landing page. You are allowed one active link in your bio. You can include other URL's in your description, but they will not be active.

- Make sure you take advantage of the reply and direct message features. These two features are the real "meat and potatoes" of Twitter. Using them will result in strong (and profitable) relationships with other users.

- Use a link shortening tool like TinyURL to shorten links to deal with the 140 character limit for each tweet.

- There are some cool third part tools which I use to ramp up Twitter's marketing potential. Be sure to see my Twitter bio for more information about this.

Give Twitter a try for a few weeks and watch the results!

About the Author

Steve Weber quit the rat race and now works full time from his home. Want to learn how you can do it too? Click here for a free   video   =>
http://www.weberinternetmarketing.com/videos/video-weber.htm

INDEX*

195

LaVergne, TN USA
18 August 2009
155048LV00006BA/396/P